Reflections

of a

Teacher's

Heart

A Compilation of Writings by

Kristen Hall

Elementary Teacher

(and so, so much more!)

Dedication Pages

Editor's note: It has been a great honor to work together to compile these "reflections" into book form. Miss Kristen M. Hall was definitely a master teacher, one from whom we all could learn. Retyping her writings has been like a refresher course in not only the "how-to's" of teaching, but also the "why's."   We offer here dedications, from Kristen's most long-time friends since college days.   These were her friends first, later colleagues and/or parents of students in her class.

May we each strive to be better tomorrow than we are today. May every word in this book point us to a closer walk with the Lord, a better understanding of those He has called us to influence, and a greater vision of what He can accomplish through us if we will but trust and obey His call.

Emily A. (Knight) Ashcraft, long-time friend, teacher of many of the same students:

Kris and I became friends in college. She was my go-to person for advice, support, or encouragement. It would remain this way for all the years we were friends. I loved that we were able to work in the same schools and ministries together. We prayed for many of the same students together. She had a soft spot for that student who just needed a chance – an opportunity to see what they could be capable of. I was one of the few adults who truly saw her teacher's heart.

I will never forget the first time I saw her in a classroom setting. She was a completely different person. Her demeanor was different, her voice was different, her stance was different; everything about her was different. Here was my friend teaching children in a classroom. Or was this someone else entirely? The students responded. They were learning and growing without resistance and without even realizing it, really.

I am a better person, a better friend, a better teacher for the privilege of having had a person like Kris for such a good friend for such a long time.

Lisa Steele Perryman, long-time friend, teacher:

My memories with Kris start back in our college days. Terri Johnson, Kris, and I worked in the Dean of Women's Office for Mrs. Marlene Evans. Carolann Capaci was Mrs. Evans' secretary, and I guess you could say we three were her "minions." In working together, we became like a little family, but for sure, lifelong friends. Kris was always the one who was quiet, hidden away typing. She was incredibly fast and accurate. I could tell she was really smart and very creative. She could sing, draw, and read a story, bringing it to life like no one else! We all could see, even then, that she had much to give; and we knew she would be a good teacher. But we had no idea how "good" because she was always such a mystery! We never dreamed that our quiet friend would touch so many lives (ours included) for which we are so thankful. She has influenced so many young lives with her love for learning, while loving them like her own children. She has opened doors of knowledge and unlocked students' minds to do and learn the things they did not think they could do. She brought the Bible stories to life and helped them with their math and English. She wanted them all to grasp the concepts and have the foundation they needed for their high school years. She encouraged them to write and believe in themselves. She made history and science fun, exciting, and adventurous! My own Micah loves our country's history and takes pride in his country because of Miss Kris' teaching.

The mystery of Kris was unlocked! You see, she became the person God called her to be. I remember the first time I listened to her teach. I marveled that this was my quiet, smart, and talented friend of so many years. She was a different person inside the classroom. It was her niche. She felt freedom to share her heart and be who she really was with our kids: a teacher. And we were all blessed for it. She gave all she had to her students. Teaching our children was what she lived for! She fought hard her last two years to continue her twenty-five plus years of making education in the classroom what it should be. She finished her race strong! She was an awesome teacher!

She loved my own children and was always very thoughtful of them. She was like a second mom to Samuel. She treasured his hugs and he thought she was always so kind. ... Not having Kris be in Samuel's life as he continues to grow up is probably the hardest part for me. Nothing means more to parents than someone loving and being good to their child. She was probably the best friend he will ever have this side of Heaven.

Heaven is an even sweeter place now that our Miss Kris is there. She is greatly missed. Our hearts feel broken at times, and we cry; but we will be with her again! I am happy for her! No more sickness or pain. I am thankful for our friendship. She was a blessing to me in many ways. I tried to be a blessing to her as well.

I love you, Kris. I miss you, and I always will. Thank you for the great memories we have shared and for being my friend.

Table of Contents

An
Introductory
Impression

*Kristen Hall taught students at two schools during her lifetime. The first, where she began her career straight out of college, was State Line Christian School (**SLCS**), in Temperance, Michigan. The second, and last, was Gospel Light Christian School (**GLCS**), in Hot Springs, Arkansas.*

Let us take just a few minutes to learn who is Kristen Hall, teacher extraordinaire. These first few entries include those from colleagues and friends who stood alongside her, shaping the generations to follow.

Mr. John Morrissey, Principal, SLCS:

A Tribute to Kris Hall

To me she will always be "Miss Hall." A master teacher in training and practice, Kris Hall always had a project going on in her class for the children to inspire wonder and imagination. Maybe the center of attention was a cocoon waiting to open, or a little living friend such as a fish or a tadpole. Kris inspired wonder in children because wonder was a living part of her own life.

In each lesson she taught, students could see in her eyes her own wonder, amazement, and interest in history, Bible, science, or any other subject. That child-like wonder and enjoyment – the interest that makes a person want to learn more – is a vital part of an excellent teacher.

I saw that smile, that pleasant, focused expression everywhere – in her day-school class and in her Sunday school class. Don't let that part of her deceive you, though. She was intense in her wonder and in how she believed a classroom should be administered.

I have seen her straightening out a problem with a student or between students. I have seen her hold her ground in frustration and courage over a conflict that interfered with her teaching or stand up to administration when it clashed with a principle for which she would just about die!

What a teacher! What a person! What a Christian! I am privileged to have known her and look forward to seeing her again.

Mrs. Margaret Yoshida, Elementary Principal, GLCS:

Kris Hall!! All who had the privilege of knowing her will remember her as an outstanding teacher and dear friend who loved and lived to please her Lord and Saviour, Jesus Christ.

Her classroom had a variety of activity centers where students could go after finishing their work. These centers covered a variety of interests such as: arts and crafts, science collections, puzzles, and games. But the one that inspired them the most was the library. Books, books, books!! She shared her own books and had the room set up with a sofa, rocking chairs, and pillows like home. Her love for books inspired the students to love reading. Even today, though many years have passed, her students remember Miss Hall's passion for the Lord and books.

Although she was battling cancer, she continued to teach until very near the end with the same testimony ... "Well done, thou good and faithful servant!"

Carolann Capaci, long-time friend, Pastor's wife, GLCS:

I met Kris Hall in 1986 when I began working for Mrs. Marlene Evans. She was one of my office workers at the time. Not only was she very talented and creative, but she was also a great writer. However, she lacked communication skills back then. When the Lord brought our paths back together years later when she came to work for Gospel Light Christian School, those skills hadn't changed much. What was different was that she was an amazing teacher, and for some reason, she had the ability to teach children to love reading and school. She made learning enjoyable. My children who are both in college at this time still feel she was their favorite teacher.

I saw my friend feel very alone while surrounded by many students and friends. As she shared this with me one Sunday afternoon, I asked her if she communicated with God easily; did she feel like God was with her? She answered, "No." She felt as if she did not know how to communicate with Him or people unless teaching them. After asking God to help me know what to say, I remember telling her to write her feelings to God. I had always known that she was excellent at writing her feelings down through stories or poems. Thus her journey began. The more she would communicate her feelings to God through journaling, and hearing Him speak to her through His Word, the more she was able to start communicating easier in all of her relationships. First with her Jesus, to Whom she became very close during her parent's passing away and through her own battle with cancer. I saw her blossom in all of her other relationships....and one of the last times I asked her if she felt alone before her passing, she beamed with a smile and said, "No!"

She used to love Eyore from Winnie the Pooh because that was the way she would feel. But towards the end of her fight with cancer, I saw her turn into a combination of Winnie the Pooh and Tigger! She was kind and loving like Winnie the Pooh and happy and carefree like Tigger! What a transformation! It all started with her close relationship with Jesus and her ability to communicate to Him.

Kris' life still lives on in her writing. I pray that you will all be blessed as you read her works in this book.

Miss Michele Stevenson, First Grade Teacher, Co-Worker, Friend, SLCS:

What can I say about Kris? She was a master teacher. I remember learning from her the art of showing gratitude. At her birthday party when it was time to open gifts, she turned the gift from being all about her to being all about the person who gave her the gift. First, she would find out who gave her the gift; then she would pull out the gift and be totally in awe of whatever it was, She would say something like: "This will be perfect on my kitchen table." When she was finished, a person felt as if he had climbed Mount Everest for her. She did that for each and every gift. From that point on, I copied her method of gift receiving whenever a student gave me a gift.

Mrs. Marlenia Sims, School Secretary, Teacher, Co-Worker, Friend,GLCS

Kris Hall was so influential in the life of the Sims family. She taught all three of my sons, and she was my co-worker. I also had the honor of taking her to some of her doctor's appointments as she battled cancer. If I could summarize Kris, I would say that she poured her life into each of her students. She wanted them to reach the potential that she saw in each of them.

Every time I use the word "sneaked" instead of the incorrect usage of "snuck" I know she is smiling and giving the head nod from Heaven. I will forever be grateful for the impact of Kristen Hall. Until we meet again, you are gone but not forgotten.

A

Glimpse

of

Home

I Miss . . .

I never knew that I would miss the home I left as much
as this

I miss my room. I miss my chair. I miss all of the pictures
there.

I miss the halfway painted house. I miss the squeaking of
the mouse

That always in my baseboard goes and sometimes runs
across my toes.

I miss the garden and the trees. I miss the flowers and
pretty leaves.

I miss the church that lacks a top because of a wind that
wouldn't stop.

But more than all of these you see, I miss my favorite
family.

I miss each one of my nephews three. I even miss my
niece-to-be.

I miss my little brother a lot, who drove my car and now
it's not.

I miss my sister, her husband, too. When at their house,
I'm at the zoo!

I also think they miss me lots, for who will babysit those
tots?

I miss my brother who's twenty-three, although him at home you'll never see.

I miss my mother and father, too. I wouldn't be here if not for you.

You're giving up a lot for me. I'll make you proud; you wait and see.

I will work hard and do my best, and then trust God to do the rest.

I miss home much, and I'll miss it more before it's time to come home, I'm sure.

I just wanted to tell you this: I like it here, but there's lots I miss . . .

My Dad

My intention was to write a poem to describe my father Charles Hall. I have fought with words for weeks, feeling limited by the constraints of rhyme and meter. So, for the present, I have postponed this pursuit of a stirring poem and have simply chosen to rely on simple words.

My Dad is the hardest worker I have ever known. It is quite rare for a person with a mind as sharp as my Dad's to not be afraid of manual labor. His industriousness has never been limited to his salaried occupation, but to every endeavor he has ever undertaken. I have early memories of him working on cars in the heat of the day, with sweat streaming off his brow. He would be drenched with perspiration yet never seemed to mind. He had a job to do.

My Dad went to work every day. He never called off for silly reasons. Idleness has never been a part of his life. Even now in retirement one can seldom find him idle.

There are many facets to my Dad's life. He is a gardener, a hunter, a deacon, a businessman, a poet, a carpenter, a songleader, a jokester (Who has not seen his *Pride and Joy?*), a giver, a designer, a philosopher, a cook (Did you ever try his Zucchini Surprise?), a chauffer, a fisherman, a grandfather, a husband, and a son. But most importantly to me, he is a father. He is someone of whom I have always been proud to say, "That's my Dad!"

Happy Birthday! I love you!   Kris

Mother's Day

I went to the store to purchase Mother's Day cards. After spending several minutes choosing the "perfect" one for my mother, my eyes were drawn to the grandmother cards.

My dad's mother is soon to be ninety-six years of age. At the present time, she is in relatively good health, living alone, and occupying her time by painting greeting cards for her friends and family. I lovingly selected a beautiful card adorned with white roses. The purchase of this card was quite precious to me, as today I fully realize that my grandmother's future Mother's Days are limited. I treasure this moment.

Did I treasure the moment last year as much as this? No. I'm wiser now. I understand that life is precious yet so fleeting. As I walked away from the card aisle, my heart wept. Today, I bought two cards for Mother's Day; last year I had selected three. How many will I purchase next year? I must cherish each relationship while I am able, for I can never be sure when that relationship will end, leaving only memories – great memories – and emptiness.

Dear Nana

I did not wish to let you go.
I wanted you to stay.
You're such a part of "who I am,"
I'm lost with you away.

I think of all you've meant to me.
Some things . . . though rather small
Did take upon a greater light
The day you left us all.

The touch of your hand, the sound of your voice,
The sparkle in your eye,
Your delightful, childlike wonder of life;
For these my heart doth cry.

I wish so much to call you back.
It's selfish . . . this I know.
But just once more to hold you close,
Before I let you go.

Dear Nana,

It has been ten whole months since you've been gone.
The emptiness still remains. Often, in my busyness I
think the emptiness has departed. And yet it is still
there, lurking beyond this present thought. I have heard
that the hurt fades, yet I am not sure that this is true.

I miss you. You are often in my thoughts and always in
my heart. I long to receive your cards for every holiday;
to accompany you on any trip; to dust your hutch for
twenty-five cents; to send you some silly socks; to warm

your cold hands. You're gone. You are never coming back. Your possessions have been dispersed. Your dog has received a new home. Your spoons, John Wayne videos, beaded ornaments, and tiger wall hanging are now in another's house. Death is final. And yet, our separation is not final. Someday, although you cannot return to me, I can come to you. The only remedy for this emptiness is the knowledge of eternal life with loved ones so dear to us. I miss you . . . for now. I'll see you again someday. Until then . . . good - bye.

Love,

Kris

I Remember

I remember the day my grandfather "Doc" died. It was a warm spring day. I was ten years old. When I arrived home from school, my mother was gone. My little brother was playing in the sandbox, and my older brother was in the house alone.

My older brother soon received a phone call from my mom. Doc was very sick. We needed to be ready to leave as soon as Dad came home from work. My brother sent me to quickly ride my bike to the junior high school to get my sister from basketball practice. I jumped on my bike and raced off on my mission. When I entered the gymnasium, my sister was mortified. Not only had I, her kid sister, interrupted her practice, but I was an appalling sight as well. I had forgotten to put on my shoes. My white knee socks were now very dirty and sagging to my ankles. I can surely understand why she was embarrassed.

Upon arriving home with my sister, my brother whispered in my ear that was Doc was dead. I felt so strange. I knew that I probably was supposed to cry, but it did not seem real. I did not feel like crying. I just felt numb. My sister and I walked into our bedroom. I knew that I needed to let her know about Doc, but I did not know quite what to say. Finally, I began to cry. My sister told me not to worry because Doc would be okay. I then let her know what our brother had said. Then we both cried.

That was the first time someone I had known and loved had passed away. Even though I had cried, I never realized how I would really feel until I went to Doc's funeral and finally to his house, where his chair remained . . . empty.

A Very Memorable Day

It was to be my first day of Bible school. I was so excited that I could hardly wait! Although I was only four, I remember this day as if it were yesterday.

My older brother, my sister, and I were scurrying about the house getting ready. Finally, it was almost time to go. But wait! We had forgotten that all important chore: brushing our teeth. We, along with our dad, rushed to the bathroom. We were all crowding around the sink. First was my dad on the left, then my brother, then my sister, and finally me. I was trying to be careful so as not to step on the diaper pail lid, which was on the floor covering a hole in the floor. This hole had been cut in the floor by my dad in order to build a laundry chute. When the chute was finished, we would be able to open the drawer and toss our dirty clothes down the chute where they would land on the laundry room floor. At this time, there was only a hole covered by the diaper pail lid.

As we feverishly brushed our teeth, I kept getting nudged closer and closer to the hole. Suddenly, my sister looked over and said, "Where's Kris?" I had silently disappeared. My dad quickly figured out what had happened. He raced downstairs as fast as his legs could carry him.

I fared better than anticipated as I landed on some dirty laundry rather than on the cement floor. All would have been fine if not for that sharp nail sticking out from the wall, which caught me on my way down.

After a few stitches at the hospital, I was almost as good as new. Dad soon made a proper laundry chute. Eventually, I did get to attend Bible school.

Where's The Salsa?

It was the first summer in my new house. I had decided to try my hand at gardening. After preparing a small section of land, I tenderly planted numerous seedlings. There were tomatoes, cucumbers, onions, peppers, and zucchini. In anticipation, I eagerly watched my garden grow.

During this time, a friend, knowing of my gardening endeavors, sent me a book about home canning. I wasn't too interested at first. Canning was something that old-timers did. I wouldn't know where to begin. Soon, my plants started to produce. That first cucumber was a work of art. I was so very proud of my little garden and relished each vegetable. But the more I thought about it, and the more produce I picked, my willingness to learn about canning grew. It didn't look quite as hard as I first thought. The salsa recipe actually looked possible. I already had most of the ingredients. With a burst of daring, I drove to the store. After much deliberation, I finally chose the proper canning supplies. At the checkout, I realized this was going to be some very expensive salsa. But I reassured myself that this was an investment. I would be making salsa for many years to come.

Labor Day was truly a day of labor. I peeled, seeded, and chopped most of the day. Following the canning book instructions carefully, step by step, I canned my first garden's produce. It was a labor of love. Those vegetables were very precious to me. I had watched them grow from seedlings. The resulting jars of salsa were even more precious. The nine perfectly sealed jars were a work of art. I was so proud. Now, I really had a grand idea. I would give each of my siblings, along with my parents and grandma, a jar of my salsa for Christmas. I visualized their reaction to such a wonderful gift. I could hardly wait.

Getting the salsa to Kansas was going to be a problem. Since I was flying home for Christmas, I couldn't take it all in my carry-on luggage. I definitely wouldn't trust it to checked baggage. How could I get it to Kansas?

Sometime in November, I received a phone call that solved my predicament. My friend from Kansas (the canning book friend) was driving up to Chicago for Thanksgiving, and if I could meet her there, she would deliver to me some Christmas gifts from my mother; and she would take back any gifts for my family. This plan would work out perfectly. We met, had lunch, exchanged gifts, and were on our way. She had instructions to deliver the salsa directly to my mother. I had cautiously left my precious jars in her care. I waited anxiously for the call from my mother, telling me that the salsa had arrived safely. The word came, and I breathed a sigh of relief.

I eagerly made plans for Christmas. I even planned the little round pieces of cloth and string to decorate the tops of my jars. I was soon ready for Christmas. The day before I was to leave for Kansas, I received alarming news from my mother. The salsa was missing. Somehow it had been misplaced. Although I wondered how someone could possibly lose five jars of salsa, I handled the news quite well. I knew that once I arrived, I would find it. On Christmas Eve, I searched every possible place in my parents' house. It was nowhere to be found. I was horribly disappointed but managed to put on a happy face. I didn't want to spoil Christmas by having a bad attitude; besides, people are more important than things, right? I was very proud of my sweet spirit. I also knew that I had almost two weeks after Christmas to tear the house apart and find my salsa!

The day to dig in finally arrived. I methodically searched every nook and cranny of every room in the entire house. You may wonder why this would be such a huge endeavor. Well, both my parents are savers. They save everything. Their house is full of odds and ends. Although it sounds incredulous, in their residence it is very possible to lose items much larger than a box of salsa. I was soon on the floor with a flashlight looking under beds, digging in closets, and tearing through the garage. Where could they be? I searched the cupboards. Maybe someone had actually placed them where the canned goods belonged. Nothing. I searched the back porch, the basement, the back bedrooms. Nothing. Although, I did find a Christmas gift that my mother had forgotten to give me, but no salsa. My father helped me search, but still, nothing. I interrogated my mother. When did she last see it? Where did she last see it? Who was the last one who touched it? Was it still in the box? Who was in the house at the time? Where was my salsa? She couldn't help me. She just didn't remember. WHAT HAPPENED

TO MY PRECIOUS SALSA??!!! Who could lose a box of salsa? What a stupid, idiotic thing to do. Didn't anybody realize how important this was to me? How stupid! How irresponsible! By now, I was tired, dirty, frustrated, and empty-handed. I left the house, fuming. Although I never said any of the harsh thoughts I was thinking, I'm sure my parents knew by my demeanor how disgusted I was.

After driving around for a while, I finally got myself under control. I had wanted so much for my salsa, something I had made myself, to be a perfect present for my family. I was terribly disappointed. I knew now that my family was not going to receive the salsa, at least not *this* Christmas.

I thought about all of the work that had gone into making that salsa. Then I considered how much work my parents had put into rearing me. I thought about all of the wonderful things they both had done for me. Suddenly, my anger melted in the realization that the greatest treasure in that house was not my salsa. I could always make more of that. These two people were the only parents I would ever have. What did some stupid salsa compare with that? People truly are more important than things, especially these people. Was I still disappointed? Yes. Did I still think it was kind of crazy? Yes. Did it matter anymore? No. Not at all. In fact, it was rather humorous. The last few days of vacation were not spent in searching for salsa but in appreciating the precious treasure of which I had almost lost sight.

The fate of the missing salsa remained a mystery until the following March. My father found the box containing the salsa just before I came home for spring break. It was in the garage all along beneath a garbage bag filled with aluminum cans. No one ever considered picking up the bag to look under it. I was able to personally deliver each jar of salsa after all. This was all perfect timing, and the lesson of the salsa was firmly imprinted on my heart.

Kris' Birthday

A lovely child,
Born in the year 1963
At Missouri Methodist Hospital
Into the Hall family.

Grew up in Lansing, Kansas.
A home we built in '60.
Falling through the laundry chute,
She was very frisky.

She loved our dog named Pokey,
Chased ducks under weeping willow.
Even had a pet cat, "Gypsy";
It had kittens on her pillow.

She likes to stand by a yard lamp,
Especially in her peach dress.
Though usually barefooted,
A Christian lady I have to confess.

She went off to college
At Hyles-Anderson to receive a
Master's Degree,
Working in Marlene Evans' office,
A teacher she wanted to be.

She now teaches at State Line,
Loves all her students, present and
past,
Instilling in them Christian principles,
A value through life that will last.

She has her own home,
Which she shares with her dog
Baylee;
Driving her own car,
They deliver papers daily.

Many things happen
As through life we go,
But today is a special day,
It's Kris' big 4 – 0.

Happy Birthday!

Love, Dad

10-25-03

A
Glimpse
of Faith

He Touched Me!

He touched me! He touched me!
He reached right in and touched me!
I came hoping to be healed;
All myself to Him did yield.
Yet never once did I imagine He would dare,
A clean and wholesome touch with me to share.
He touched me!

Many years had passed since I felt one gentle touch
From anyone of whom I could call friend.
I remember well the day when I at first was cast away.
Such despair no one can comprehend.
Destined to live my life alone;
To bear my burden on my own,
Unclean, unwanted, and to misery condemned.
Then Jesus touched me!

He touched the blind man, this is true,
The deaf, the lame, the infirmed, too.
Yet, to touch one such as I
All rules and reason to defy.
To reach where no one else would ever dare,
This overwhelms my every sense.
Such love I see in evidence.
What mercy and omnipotence!
He touched me!

*". . . behold, a man full of leprosy, who seeing Jesus fell
on his face, and besought him, saying,
Lord, if thou wilt, thou canst make me clean.
And He put forth His hand, and touched him,
saying, I will: be thou clean . . . "*
Luke 5:12-13

Autumn

The leaves are turning, turning, turning.

My heart is yearning, yearning, yearning

For the warmer days and nights we had in June.

The leaves are falling, falling, falling.

The wind is calling, calling, calling;

Telling me that colder days are coming soon.

Aloneness

Just having you and your thoughts alone.

Not worrying how you look or what other people think.

Being away from the noise and bustle of people.

. . . This is aloneness.

loneliness

being alone when you're in a crowd.

having no one to talk to when there's people all around.

being near the noise and laughter but not being a part.

. . . this is loneliness

"Steadfast in His Strength"

Senior Song 1982

Though we are not certain how much, if any, of this selection was written by Kristen or her classmates, we include it in her collection because she did. It was obviously important to her. I am sure she shared this with her many classes.

So many years we wondered why God made us as we
are.
We did not understand the plan He had for us thus far.
But we have learned that He will stay beside us for the
length,
If we will only seek to follow Steadfast in His Strength.

CHORUS
Steadfast in His strength, this we long to be.
Steadfast in His work, 'til His face we see.
Living by His Holy Word, yes, this is the key.
To follow Steadfast in His Strength and live eternally.

The happiness we have today is not as others claim,
For treasure in this earthly life is not our lifelong aim.
To live a life that pleases God; this is our worthwhile
goal.
So Steadfast in His Strength we tread while living here
below.

CHORUS

We pray that by this song you'll learn what God has done for us.

He gave His only Son to die upon a rugged cross.

For with His blood He paid the price and freely did forgive.

He gave His life on Calvary, and through His Strength we live.

CHORUS

Dear Lord,   *(June 1983)*

Please help me to live this day
In such a way
As if to say,
"I love you, Lord."

Please help me to give of me;
A servant be
That they might see
I love you, Lord.

Please help me to show the way;
This every day
So others say,
"I love you, Lord."

My Captor   (1980)

My feelings are inside me,
I cannot let them show.
My insides must stay secret.
My heart no one must know.

But then again, it may be good,
To let my feelings out.
Sometimes I think I will explode.
I want to scream and shout!

I don't like being tied up.
I want to be set free.
My captor will not loosen,
The bonds he's set on me.

I'm crying, but no tears flow.
The pain is all inside.
Where can I get away to?!!
Where can I go to hide?!!

My captor's always with me.
He will not set me free.
I cannot leave his side,
Because my captor's me.

To My Friend

God brought our lives together.
What a wonderful start!
One who knows my inner soul
Yet never will depart.

Someone to listen . . . to really hear
The babbling of my heart.
To make someone feel needed,
This truly is an art.

One who desires to be with me,
Who enjoys my company.
Yet one who's fun to be around
With coffee or with tea.

To answer my unending questions
Yet never a smirk to see.
Not disregarding the little things
And caring about the "real" me.

One who possesses such wisdom
From whom I always may learn.

Who makes me feel so special,
Who shows such real concern.

A hug, a pat, a caring touch,
For this contact I do yearn.

Someone who honestly loves me.
This love can never be earned.

'Tis a wonderful season to reveal the reason
That my friend and I shan't part.
No matter the season, 'tis always this reason . . .
My friend is in my heart.

A

Glimpse

of

Friendship

Friendships

Psalm 78:12-41

Friendships are relationships and relationships take work.

I'm too busy! What motivates me?

"For He remembered that they were but flesh; a wind that passeth away, and cometh not again. How oft did they provoke him in the wilderness, and grieve him in the desert! Yea, they turned back and tempted God, **and limited the Holy One** *of Israel."*   *Psalm 78:39-41*

I.   God delights to use us.

II.   We have the power to limit an omnipotent God.

   A. By stubbornness

   B. By disobedience

III.   God desires to control our personal life.

   A. Health direct result:

   1. Limiting the days of my life or the life of my days.

   2. Energy level

   B. Comfort zone – introvert / extrovert

IV.   Who loses when we limit God?

V.   Faith

     A. Deeper trust in God

     B. Closeness in family devotions

     C. Friends

     D. Say "Good-Bye" with no regrets

     E. Tears (Jeremiah 29)

        1. Ladies' Meeting

        2. Staff Retreat

The bottom line is: I do not want to waste my life – I do not want to limit what God can do for and through me.

Are You a True Friend?

A friend is someone who knows you almost as well as you know yourself. By just a glimpse of your eye, a friend will know whether you have had a great day or a horrible one. This friend can also sense when you are tired, hurt, or frustrated. A true friend is someone who wants you to be the best you possible. This person is encouraging whenever you are faced with a daunting task and cautious when you are inching forward to a bad decision. A friend is one who loves you for who you are and is content to help you grow to be a better you. To have a genuine friend is truly a gift from God.

Are you a true friend?

Get Hard!!!   *(May 1983)*

They cannot hurt you if you're hard.
Their words will never sting.
The snide remarks won't make you cry.
You'll never feel a thing.
Get Hard!

Their talk of you behind your back
Won't phase you . . . not at all.
Those hateful things they say to you
Will just bounce off your wall.
Get Hard!

Whatever things they do to you,
Whatever words they say,
Just grit your teeth and never care.
Yourself you won't betray.
Get Hard!

BUT . . .

When you get hard, you cannot feel
A friend's soft, gentle touch.
You cannot see a sunset bright;
The hardness blinds you much.
You cannot hear the "I love you"
Of friends so close and dear.
You're torn apart betwixt the two:
Be hard or shed a tear.

The Successful Backseat Driver

The success of a backseat driver is never achieved by accident. This success is only developed by years of experience and training. Every veteran motorist has come into contact with a backseat driver at one time or another in his lifetime. This experienced driver has often marveled at the accomplishments of the successful back seat driver.

For a backseat driver to be a success, he must possess naturally quick reflexes. These reflexes include jumping at any sudden noise or movement. This ability alone does not qualify a person as a backseat driver unless the quick reflex is accompanied by loud gasps, deep sighs, or shrill screams. Taking hold of the seat in front of them is always a prime example of the demonstration of such quick reflexes. Therefore, being rapid to respond in any situation is an important attribute of the successful backseat driver.

An accomplished backseat driver is an expert navigator. He knows the choicest route to any destination and the correct speed to drive this route. One eye is always on the speedometer while the other is on the road. In any event, the backseat driver never fails to "help" the motorist by giving him useful advice on every aspect of his driving.

Consequently, learning all the attributes of successful backseat driving takes years of individualized training. Special teachers must be accomplished backseat drivers themselves. The instructors must also be good examples whereby others may emulate them. The backseat driver's teaching seemingly takes place by osmosis.

Being a successful backseat driver requires much work, skill, and perseverance.   Not everyone is qualified. Therefore, backseat driving is truly an art. However, it is interesting to note that most experienced motorists prefer to travel alone.

Take Another Lap

Editor's Note: This article was published in the "Christian Womanhood" in 1989.

"Turn right? ... This exit? ... Are you sure? ... That's what you said the last time!" I really can't believe this. She said she knew where to go. We've only been driving around in circles for the past two hours, and what's more, it is five o'clock in the morning! Why can't she get her act together?

Do those sound like Christian thoughts to you? Not on your life! I am a Christian, and those just happened to be my thoughts; but believe me, those thoughts originating from my brain were anything but Christian.

My good friend Emily and I were supposedly taking a leisurely trip. The purpose of this trip was to relax. Obviously, things were not going quite as planned. After being behind the wheel of the car for fifteen continuous hours, I was not too excited about extending my trip circling Indianapolis.

At first, I proved myself to be a patient and understanding friend. I even amazed myself with encouraging comments such as, "I know you'll remember soon," "I'm sure this is probably the right road," and, best of all, "Don't worry about it, Emily; this could happen to anyone."

Two hours later my "Christianity" seemed to have worn very thin. The silence in the car became ominous. There was nothing left for us to say. She knew I was upset. I knew I was upset. What else was there to discuss? After all, we both knew what a total idiot she was.

With much assistance, we finally made it to our destination, no thanks to Emily's great logistical abilities.

Back on the road again after a brief rest, Emily ventured forth with the question I had been waiting for: "Kris, are you still mad at me?"

I was ready with my pre-planned, philosophical answer. "I'm not really mad; I just hope you've learned your lesson so that this doesn't ever happen again. Next time you might not have someone as understanding as I." Thinking back over these pious words, I feel myself getting nauseous.

When you come right down to it, what is more important – two hours of sleep or one good friend?

If Emily would have ever asked me if I would be willing to give up two hours of sleep for her, you know my answer would have been, "Yes." I would have said yes and meant it sincerely. Why, then, was I not willing to give it up unasked?

What is the actual meaning of friendship anyway? What is a real friend worth? What is the intrinsic value of a true friend?

Emily, I was mad, extremely mad; but I was wrong, and I am very, very sorry. I certainly value our friendship more, much more than two hours of sleep or a few gallons of gas. Thank you for being such a true friend.

And, Emily, if you ever want, I will even take another lap with you around Indianapolis.

A Friend Like You

Editor's Note: This is intended to be to Renee, one of Kristen's close friends from Lewis Avenue Baptist Church, from Kristen's parents.

We thank you for your visits.
From our home we did go
To your church and our daughter
In Michigan and Ohio.
    It's nice to have a friend like you.

We went out to eat lunch.
A big meal we did scoop.
While you had only
A small bowl of soup.
    It's nice to have a friend like you.

For drinks at lunch,
We had tea and Coke.
You with your coffee,
Listening to an occasional, silly joke.
    It's nice to have a friend like you.

Then, after shopping,
Baskin-Robbins … at last!
Each of us had ice cream,
And you a Cappuccino Blast.
    It's nice to have a friend like you.

At home, we appreciate your cards,
A wonderful, communicative device.
Yours, with subjects we enjoy,
In your writings so precise.
    It's nice to have a friend like you.

We'll see you again,
Someplace, another day.
It's nice to know that we
Have a friend called Renee.
It's nice to have a friend like you.

God bless you.

A
Glimpse of
Learning

Excuse Me, May I Interrupt?

I have spoken with people who went to Bible college in order to learn how to better influence others. They themselves were greatly affected by someone, and they truly desired to reach others in the same manner. Some people I know went to Bible college in order to fulfill their life's dream of becoming a preacher or a teacher. I, myself, went to Bible college to find out if God was for real. I did not realize that Bible college was to prepare a person for full-time Christian service. I'm not sure I even knew what full-time service was. I so wanted to find something that was real, not some religion that a person would have to fake, something with a lot of rules but no substance. When I had attended a youth conference earlier in my teen years, I thought I had sensed something different at that conference. So now that it was time to attend college, I chose the place that contained my highest hopes of finding the reality of God.

I entered the doors of that institution terrified and alone. I had so many questions. Would I finally be able to find the answers to those questions? If I did find God to be real, did He want to be a part of my life? Did He have a purpose in creating me? Was I of any value to Him? Could He use me at all? I wanted so much to know. Yet, I could never find the words to ask the questions. There were people along the way who attempted to be of help. They truly did try, but I think that I must have frustrated them. I prayed that God would somehow show me the answers that I craved.

I begged Him not to give up on me. I was sure that He was tired of messing with me, yet I begged Him to give me more time to figure it out.

I struggled through. It truly was amazing that I ever made it to my senior year. My grades were fine, yet my frustrations had grown until I finally decided there was no hope. I would just finish and then return home. Obviously, I hadn't found what I had been searching. I was majoring in education, yet I knew that I could never teach. Communication was a major weak point in my life. How could I ever be able to communicate for a living? In my heart, I had given up. This was my mindset as my senior year began.

One day, I went to the Dean of Women's office. My freshman roommate was having a hard time; she was terribly homesick. She had been telling me the previous evening that the secretary of the Dean of Women had asked her how she was doing. When I asked her how she had responded, she replied, "Great!"

What a liar! I knew the truth. Therefore, I embarked on my mission to inform this concerned lady that my roommate was not doing as well as she had claimed. On that day, I had no other motive when entering that office. I had no desire to "talk" to this secretary about anything other than my roommate. Besides, she would never be able to help me. This was her first year on staff at the college. We had been in the same freshman class. She had graduated a year ahead of me only due to my having a year-long "vacation" in the middle of my junior year. Remember, I was now a senior. I was supposed to have my act all together. At least, that it is what most people would assume.

As I entered the office, the phone was ringing. This place was a beehive of activity. The lady motioned for me to sit down, and I complied. When there was a break in the action, she inquired of me what it was that I needed. I explained the situation regarding my roommate. She thanked me, and I was finished. Or, was I? This young lady then made the decision to reach out of her world and enter mine. How did she do it? Actually, it was quite simple. She asked me how I was doing. Then, she waited for me to answer. I know that it seems crazy, but with that little kindness, she changed the entire direction of my life. How could something so seemingly insignificant make such a drastic impact? Let me try to explain.

I do not remember what we talked about that day. What I do know is that it was nothing "deep." She was just interested in what I was thinking. At one point in our early conversations, on a particularly busy afternoon, she actually turned off her phone. She turned the ringer off on the phone to the Dean of Women's office! Could what I might have to say actually be of such value? Never had I felt such encouragement to share my heart.

Did the first-year staff member have all the answers? No. Did she come up with some great theological solution to my fear and uncertainty? No. What she did was something that anyone is qualified to do, yet so many fail to see the need.

1. She reached out of her world and entered mine.
2. She took the time to care.
3. She encouraged me.

When I faced something of which I was not sure, she made me feel as if I could do it. She made me believe that she believed in me. That made me believe in me, too. Encouragement is empowering. This was crucial in my upcoming months of student teaching.

Did God place her in my path at the just the right time? I'm sure that He did. But, if she had been so busy that day that she had looked right through me, I might today be working a secular job, never knowing how close I came to being blessed immeasurably with the life God had planned for me. And what would have become of the four hundred students whom I have loved and encouraged seven hours a day for 170+ days? Could someone else have given them what they needed? What if that first-year staff member had been so occupied with things that day that people became an interruption? Isn't that how we are? We have so much to do. It is hard to get it all finished. When a student comes by, do we give them our full attention? Do we look them in the eye? Do we even see them? Do we listen for real answers to our "How are you doing?" Or do we even desire a true answer? Reaching into another's life may take time. We do still have work to do, don't we? How long does it take to change a person's life anyway?

When I reflect back to my college years, that day in the office was truly a watershed in my life. Sitting next to that desk, I learned many valuable lessons which I use today. I am eternally grateful for what she did for me that day. And yet, she did benefit as well. For you see, in the next few years, I may get to teach her children. I might even get to teach yours. And I am a GOOD teacher!

Thank You

Thank you for seeing something dwelling inside.
This something 'round others was easy to hide.
You looked for a door, then discovered the key.
You opened my heart and found the real me.

I was there all the time, but no one could see.
I'd been hiding so long that I almost fooled me.
You saw something different; I still don't know why.
Could it have been something you glimpsed in my eye?

I thought I was happy; my life was well-planned.
I didn't need anyone; it was all in my hands.
You then knocked on my door. How could you have
dared?
I could ignore anyone except someone who cared.

And so you endeavored with attention quite rapt,
To take on the challenge of potential untapped.
You had glimpsed something there you thought
worthwhile to save;
So you worked and you loved and you cared and you
gave . . .

Of your time, (which is one thing you've never enough,
For yourself, your work, and all of that stuff),
Time for the tangibles, evidence to bear,
That this was for real. You truly did care.

You chiseled and chipped; soon you caused me to melt.
You then found a heart where an iceberg once dwelt.
But the work 'twasn't easy, sometimes quite intense;
For you see, I was trained with a well-kept defense.

I've pushed you away when fear entered my heart
And said, "She's too close, push her out if you're smart."
And still you'd come back with a welt on your cheek
Where the emotional slap landed only last week.

You've shown self-control; this I have to admit.
And giv'n no reaction when pushed to the limit.
I've not made it easy; sometimes it's been rough.
Yet you never quit going when the going got tough.

You've seen all the tears which resided inside,
Which did not yet dare to glisten the eye.
And you've shown that loving is the best way to live;
That giving your heart is the best way to give.

You've accepted me for whatever I was.
That's a very rare thing which a rare person does.
Giving courage to launch out, but still giving slack
And a cushion to land on when I sort of fall back.

You've spotted the little and made it a lot.
You say that I'm growing when I think I'm not.
Your words of encouragement must be part of a plan,
For with each word I'm stronger, for I then think I CAN.

You've been a real person - not perfect - but real;
So that in your humanity, I somehow can feel
There's something attainable, something to obtain,
A lively ambition which fear shan't enchain.

You've forced me to do that impossible task,
And then something worse, you forced me to ask
For whatever I needed. It seems simple, I know;
But with all you've commanded, you've helped me to
grow.

You've taken my independence and transferred it to
One
Whom I could depend on – this one, the Son,
While by-stepping a dangerous ground to pass through,
That well-known danger of clinging to you.

You've been a true friend, a counselor, and guide,
Yet you drew me toward One Who'll always abide.
Knowing if on you I grew to depend,
When time came for parting, my growing would end.

So now I know God more than ever I dreamed.
I see new perspective each day now it seems.
I know that He sent you and gave you the key
To unlock my chains and help set me free.

He gave you the wisdom to see something more;
He gave you the knowledge to know the right door.
He gave you His love and a goal to achieve;
This goal was quite evident as in me you believed.

I'll not take for granted the time which you've spent.
God sent you to help me; 'twas no accident.
I'll grasp what you've shown me; and then I'll begin
To help someone who needs me, who's now where I've
been.

Thank you for listening and going His way,
And believing in me yesterday and today.

Ugh! It's a Worm!

I love the smell of spring, especially after a soaking rain. The whole world looks and smells clean and bright. The birds are chirping; the trees are budding (almost as if before my very eyes); puffy clouds are floating across a deep blue sky; and a cool, soft breeze is blowing. There is nothing like a cool spring morning. At least these were my thoughts one morning until . . . it happened. I looked down.

Since I had been gazing up at the clouds and trees, I had failed to see the ground beneath my shoes. The sidewalk was covered with earthworms. Surely you have seen them after a heavy rain. During the downpour, the worms come up out of the ground and try to cross the sidewalk using the water as a lubricant. They no sooner get halfway across when the rain stops. They go a little further, but as soon as the pavement starts to dry, the worms are in trouble. They are stranded in the middle of the sidewalk, and soon they begin to dry up, too.

When most people happen to see one of these helpless creatures, they usually exclaim, "Ugh! A worm!" They continue on their way, walking cautiously in order to avoid squishing one, not for the sake of the worm, but rather for the sake of their clean shoes.

I would never think of telling anyone my feelings on the matter. I would be too embarrassed. When I see a worm in this predicament, I wait until no one is looking, pick it up, and place it back in the nice, wet grass. Whenever anyone finds out, they usually laugh at me. I know. I guess I am being silly, but I can't help it. I just hate to see that poor worm lying there drying up.

This morning the predicament of the worms bothered me more than usual. By the time I came upon them, the sun had already been doing its work. The sidewalk was almost dry and so were the worms. Of all those sad creatures I saw (and believe me, there were plenty) I could only rescue two; and it was doubtful as to whether they would survive. I was close to tears when I came to the end of my walk.

Why did it bother me so much? Why should some stupid, slimy worms drying up bother me? I guess it is because so many times in my life I have found myself in a similar predicament. I have let myself slip into a situation in which I seemed, at first, to be in control. I just followed the crowd. No one forced me; I did it on my own. It was my own decision. Then, suddenly, the tables turned. Things didn't end up as I had planned. I was stuck. I was stranded in the middle of nowhere, and I did not have the strength to pull myself out. I needed someone to reach out and help me along those last few remaining inches to safety. In such a situation, I think it would practically destroy me if someone capable of helping me were to jump back and exclaim, "Ugh! A worm!" I don't know if worms have feelings, but even if they don't, I still want to keep picking them up and putting them back in the grass. Even if it doesn't really help them, it sure does help me. It reminds me that there are a lot of people who get stranded in life, and they just need a kind hand to reach out to help them.

Whenever I should happen to come across such a one, I will fail to notice them if I'm too busy gazing at the sky. Once I see them, I could never have the heart to say, "Ugh! A worm!" knowing, once upon a time, I was one myself.

"No!"

As a child, I was not the most athletic person in the classroom. I could hold my own in most games, although I was definitely not known for my athletic prowess. Beginning in fourth grade, a new program was added to our physical education class. This was known as the President's Physical Fitness Test. This became a test that I would dread in the coming years. It's not that I was a wimp. I would do my best. When performing the six-hundred-yard run, I would run the entire time. I would never walk. I might not have ever won, but I was never last, and I definitely never quit. I gave my all to every event.

The one event that was to be my downfall was the flexed arm hang. In order to pass this test, a girl had to grip a bar suspended above her head, pull herself up until her chin was even with the bar, and then remain in that position for a certain number of seconds. When I first saw this done in fourth grade, I didn't think it looked too difficult. Looks were deceiving. I was shocked as my turn came, and I found that I was unable to even pull myself up into the proper position. I tried and tried and tried. I had miserably failed this part of the test. I am sure that I was not the only failure that day, but that did not ease the sting.

I practiced the flexed arm hang many times in the following months on the old swingset in the back of our home. I was never able to accomplish even the pulling up part. I did not want to get another "zero seconds" the next year, but I did. This continued for the next three years. I really did try, but I never succeeded.

How much humiliation can one person experience before they have had enough? I'm sure you are aware that children tend to be cruel to those who cannot do what everyone else seems to be able to do. This is especially true during those junior high years. How many times is a person to try to do something before it is obvious that they are only going to fail again? Needless to say, I dreaded the President's Physical Fitness Test each year. Nevertheless, it kept coming.

Finally, eighth grade rolled around. Only this year, P.E. had a new twist. Not only did we have a man for a teacher, but the entire class was co-ed. This truly was not a good situation.

When it came time for that infamous President's Physical Fitness Test, I dismally wondered when the flexed arm hang would be scheduled. How many times would I have to fail before they would realize that I really could not do this activity? How many times would I have to suffer this humiliation?

Finally, the day I had been dreading arrived. I had decided that I had had enough. I intentionally left my gym clothes at home that morning. I wondered if I would get in trouble. I had never done anything like that before. But that was not all. I was not going to be humiliated again. I was **not** going to do the flexed arm hang.

Now, you must understand something. I was a good kid. I always tried to do whatever my teachers wanted me to do. I had never, ever defied them. I wanted to please them. Isn't that what you are supposed to do? But I knew that I could not handle the humiliation even one more time.

One by one, our names were alphabetically called. As Mr. Scott came near to the H's, my heart raced. Finally, it was my turn. When he called my name, I said, "No." For the first time in my life, I had told a teacher "No." He then looked at me and called my name a second time. Again, I replied, "No." My teacher then went on quietly through the list. I now felt sure that I was facing the fiery pit. I knew that my parents would soon be called, and I would be facing expulsion. What an impudent act -- to defy your teacher! I wondered what Mr. Scott would do.

If you were that teacher that day, what would you have done? If I were that teacher, what would I have done? Defying the teacher is the number one, big bad no-no. Yet, it does happen. And when it does, are we ready for it? Often we want to take it personally. How dare that child defy me? Doesn't he realize that he has to obey me? My authority is at stake. If a child will directly disobey my instructions, what will the other children think? What will the other children do? My reputation is on the line. Besides, now I am mad.

When a teacher takes the child's defiance personally and reacts in anger, he makes a tragic mistake. I am not saying that defiance ought not to be punished. It should be, especially if it is a recurrent event. But we punish the child for the benefit of that child, not to validate the authority of the teacher. When teachers press the issue, they stand to lose far more than they ever stand to gain. It never pays to have a showdown in the classroom.

What is a teacher to do? I firmly believe that first of all, I must consider the child. Is this a recurring problem, or is this out of character for this child? Am I seeing the entire picture? I am not saying that you ought to excuse bad behavior. I am saying that you ought to try to understand "out of the ordinary" behavior.

Children are still learning. Often they will say "No" because they are backed into a corner, and they don't know what else they can say. Honestly, as an eighth grader, I did not realize that I could have gone to the teacher earlier to explain my dilemma. I had not yet learned the art of making an appeal. At that time, I had no other option open to me that I knew of. So, I said, "No."

What did Mr. Scott do? As he dismissed the class, he told me to stay behind. Now the class knew that I did not get away with it. It was none of their business what my punishment was. He mercifully looked beyond my defiance and saw my frustration. He told me that he understood but that I still needed to try. That kind man had me attempt one more time to do the flexed arm hang, but this time with a new twist. I didn't have to pull myself up. I only had to hang on. He would time me in that position.

He didn't give me a lecture. He didn't call my parents. In fact, he never referred to the incident again. Today I appreciate Mr. Scott's wisdom and compassion. He kindly corrected an erring child with mercy. I am not saying to disregard the rules and policies of the school. I am only saying to use wisdom in discerning what is really happening.

The Headband Story

I've heard that when going through a difficult situation, a person is not to ask "Why?" Asking "What am I supposed to learn from this?" is the proper question. While at college, I was faced with just such a situation. I'm not sure that I have totally learned the lesson. But I am definitely more aware, and I try to be more thoughtful of other people.

I had completed two and a half years of college. Then I went home for a year. Near the end of that year, while preparing to return to school, I found that I needed major surgery on my head. I had a growth that had completely filled up one of the sinus cavities in my forehead. In order to remove the growth, an incision would be made starting at one temple, going across the top of my forehead, and ending at the other temple. The incision would be made under the hairline to avoid dealing with a Frankenstein-like scar on my forehead for the rest of my life. So, two inches of my hair was shaved off, from ear to ear across the top of my head. While dreading the entire prospect, I knew I had no other choice. The surgery was successful. I knew that eventually the hair would grow back.

When the new semester began, I went ahead and returned to school. I wore a headband to cover the scar and missing hair. I tried to make the headband as inconspicuous as possible. I wore it under my hair and tried to coordinate it as best I could to match whatever outfit I would be wearing. I thought I was ready to meet the world. I was wrong.

While at home, everyone who knew me was aware of the reason for the headband. At school, it was a different story. Most people thought I was trying to be "cool." They saw me dressing differently and decided I was a rebel, trying to prove something. Very few people asked why I wore the headband. In fact, I can't think of anyone who did. But many people, mostly teachers and staff members, made acidic comments about my headband. I remember being so frustrated not only that they were misunderstanding me, but also that I was not even getting the opportunity to defend myself. I couldn't really make a sandwich sign that read: "Please be patient. I had surgery. I'm really not trying to be cool." (Anyone who really knows me will laugh at the thought of my trying to be cool. I haven't got a cool bone in my body.) People whom I respected greatly were disgusted with me. I was at a loss. I didn't know how to handle the situation.

Eventually, word did get around; and some people found out the truth. Many people to this day still think I was this strange rebel who was trying to prove something. Since leaving college, I have met up with several people from school who wonder why I no longer wear my headband. I just tell them that I don't need it any longer since my hair grew back. That usually sets them back a bit.

So often we look at people and think we know why they do what they do. We are so quick to judge. There are times that we may be correct, but most of the time, we are so wrong. As I said, I haven't, by any means mastered this. But I do know how it feels to be condemned unjustly. I appeal to you: when next you see someone who looks or dresses in a strange way or who does something that seems really weird to you, ask yourself, "Do I really have all the facts?" We need to give each other a break, take off the magnifying glasses, and reach out with a helping hand. We may find out that maybe, just maybe, we might be missing something.

Letter to a Teacher

This letter was found in Kristen's notebook with the obituary notice for Mrs. Suzann Brune.

The article lists Mrs. Brune's date of death as December 4, 2000, and the letter is dated for February. So, although she did not ever see it, may it serve here as a tribute to every Mrs. Brune and every Miss Hall: true teachers who truly inspire the leaders of the next generation.

May every student be blessed to have at least one such teacher in their life.
And may this letter also serve here as a reminder to us to thank them.

Dear Mrs. Brune:

This letter has been long overdue. I've thought of writing it for many years, but thoughts don't seem to get the job done . . .

I was in your third grade class in 1973. I don't know how well you remember me. (I can only imagine how many students you've had since then.) But, I remember you very well. While in my freshman year of college, I was required to write a paper describing a teacher that made an impression on my life. I had two teachers that I was able to mention. You were one.

Thank you for making me feel like you cared about me. I'm not sure if you thought I was anything special, but you made me feel like you did. I loved your class, even though I hated writing spelling words zillions of times. I loved it that you took time to play kickball and softball with us. I know of no other teacher that did that. The game seemed to work better (less fights, more fairness) when the teacher pitched.

You also were the only teacher who ever gave me a hug. In fact, yours was the only hug I remember getting at that time of my life. Thank you. That hug meant a lot. With society the way it is today, it is quite sad that that hug would not be allowed.

Today, I teach fourth grade at a Christian school in Michigan. I think about you often. I kind of thought you might want to know that I do remember you and that you did make a difference. Thank you.

Sincerely,

Kristen M. Hall

P.S.   I bought a *Trouble* game for my class last Christmas. I play with them at recess and think of you . . .

A

Glimpse

of

Teaching

The Definition of an Idiot

Children never cease to amaze me. Their sincerity and honesty cannot be equaled.

Scott, a five-year-old from the local pre-school where I worked, reflected that honesty in his bright, blue eyes. These eyes revealed the complete trust he held in adults. We were having "free play" when Scott seemed to need some personalized attention. I had a "bright" idea and challenged him to a puzzle race. Scott seemed enthusiastic as we chose our puzzles. For mine, of course, I chose one with a little more detail to compensate for the age difference.

"On your mark, get set, go!" I said.

Scott and I raced feverishly to replace our pieces. My airplane puzzle was soon giving me "fits." I was struggling to replace a cloud when the room grew still. I glanced up to see Scott's impish grin. He had finished and was eager to help me, much to my humiliation.

"This piece goes here, Teacher," he said.

Being beaten by a five-year-old was enough to crush my ego. To have him sincerely want to help me was more than I could stand.

I grumbled, "Scott, I think I can do it myself. I'm not an idiot, you know." Scott's innocent blue eyes grew wide in dismay as he replied, "I know you're not an idiot, Teacher. An idiot is someone who pulls out in front of you and slows down."

The Key to Learning

As a teacher, I have many things that I desire to give to each one of my students. I want them not only to learn, but also to obtain a love for learning. I yearn to instill in them a hunger to know God, and to find the perfect path which God has chosen for them. Each child must learn how to control himself, how to get along with others, and how to respect everyone -- adult and child alike. I hope to inspire my students to notice God's creation and to gain an appreciation of the intricacies of the universe. These are but a few of the truths and skills that I desire for my class to obtain.

Yet, how can I open the door to the will of the child? How can I get each child to willingly open that massive gate? For you see, only the child himself can open that door. I cannot force a child to learn. The information I yearn to give must go deeper than the mind. It must reach the heart.

A teacher might try to inspire a student to learn by catching the interest of that boy or girl with interesting facts. Every instructor should try to do this. Yet, interesting methods and information, as important as they may be, are not the key to a child's heart.

A teacher might try to reward a child who learns and punish a child who fails to try. Nevertheless, while this philosophy may have its place, the learning will only go just beneath the surface. Yes, the child may learn enough to advance to the next grade, but I want to give my students more than that.

Some educators use humor as a tool of keeping the attention of the class. While humor does have its place in the classroom, it falls short of opening the door which I seek.

Other teachers use the Bible in an attempt to shame the errant student into submission. Scripture verses and principles are thrown at a child in an attempt to correct bad behavior. Do not misunderstand. The knowledge of Bible truth is vital to the development of young minds and hearts. Yet, Bible principles given to a closed door profit about as much as seed sowed on the hard, stony ground. I cannot force the door open. I cannot beat the door down.

What is a teacher to do? I have so much to offer my students. Yet, how can I make each child willing to receive it?

There is only one key that will open the door to that inner chamber of a child's will. That key is the same key which God used to reach us all.

"For God so loved the world, that he gave his only begotten Son, that whosoever believeth in him should not perish, but have everlasting life." John 3:16

He loved us, and He showed us that unfathomable love by sending His only Son to die for us. We did not deserve it. We did not earn it. He just gave it to us freely.

The key to my students' hearts is my love for them. A child who knows he is loved will willingly open that so important door, and through that door all manner of learning may enter. Do you want your students to learn information? Love them! Do you want your students to learn to have self-control? Love them! Do you want your students to learn to accept the Bible with a hungry heart? Love them! Do you want to inspire your students not to waste their lives? Love them! By loving your students, you open a door whereby vast amounts of knowledge may enter.

You may wonder how a teacher could possibly love every student when some of them are difficult to even like. That annoying boy who picks on the other children, could I love him? That little girl whose parents rub me the wrong way, could I really love her? No. By yourself, in your own flesh, you could never love each child consistently with the depth of love that every student needs. If you want to effectually reach into a child's life, you must pray often for God to give you His love for every child and for God to love that boy or girl through you.

This love must come from God in order to be real. A child can tell the difference. He can sense when a teacher truly loves him. This is something which is impossible to fake. If teachers would faithfully petition God for His love to flow through them, miracles can occur in the classroom.

Therefore, when a child recognizes that his teacher truly loves him, he will throw open the door of his heart, allowing a multitude of truths to rush in. Do you want that unruly child to obey? Love him! Do you want that struggling girl to keep trying? Love her! Do you desire for every child under your influence to absorb the truths you are trying to impart? Love them! Be a teacher who truly makes a difference in the heart and mind of a child. Love that child. True love can never be wasted, nor can it ever be more than enough.

There is one warning for the teacher who utilizes this vital key to open up the sealed door to a child's will. When a child opens his heart, he is giving his teacher a valuable trust. Be careful that you, as a teacher, only allow those things which are just and right to enter therein; for a child whose heart is open will accept almost anything. It is now the teacher's responsibility to guard that opening. For a misused key in the hands of a careless teacher could bring disaster.

Be a successful teacher! Make a lasting difference in the lives of your students. Love them!

"Beloved, let us love one another: for love is of God; and every one that loveth is born of God, and knoweth God. He that loveth not knoweth not God; for God is love. In this was manifested the love of God toward us, because that God sent His only begotten Son into the world, that we might live through him. Herein is love, not that we loved God, but that he loved us, and sent his Son to be the propitiation for our sins. Beloved, if God so loved us, we ought also to love one another." I John 4:7-11

The Diamond

It was a small diamond.
It was not the best, nor the brightest;
Yet it was a diamond, nonetheless.

It was hiding beneath a rock amidst the mud and mire.
How it got there is inconsequential.

How it might get out is what really mattered.
For why would anyone ever think to reach into that
slime
Unless they were aware of the value contained within?

Therefore, the diamond struggled to shine.
Just a little sparkle might do.

It would try to reflect just a tiny ray of sunlight.
With all its might, it tried to catch the attention of the
passers-by.

Yet day followed day, and night followed night,
With the diamond hidden so close to view.

It longed so much for someone, anyone,
To crouch down, reach into that slimy grit,
And pry it free from its confines.

If it could get free,
It would shine with every facet of its being.
It would, it could,
But first it needed a helping hand.

Talk to Me!

"Why won't you talk to me?" "Why didn't you let me know?" "Why didn't you tell me?!!!" I've heard it all my life. But … I did tell you; you just weren't listening.

I know … what I had to say at the time didn't seem important … just a child's senseless prattle. But … don't you realize … those words were important to me?

If you do not listen to the minor, somewhat trivial things I have to say, how can I know that I can trust you with the big things? How can you judge what is big or little, important or unimportant? Some of the things I say may seem trivial, but in reality, these words are very important; for they are little clues that reveal my heart. I was talking. You just weren't listening.

You say that you know me … but you don't … not really. You know the me that lives on the outside, but you have yet to meet the me that dwells on the inside … the real me. I want to let you in. I want to open up to you. I want to talk. I need you …

I know you are busy. So many things want your attention. I also know that what I have to say may seem little and unimportant compared with other things in your life right now … but … don't be fooled. It is important.

Someday that "little" will grow big … big enough so that it will demand your attention. You will then in frustration say, "Why didn't you tell me?" But … I did … you just weren't listening.

Am I Missing Something?

Although my nephew Jacob is as mischievous and energetic as most typical four-year-olds, his green eyes often betray a deep, quiet thoughtfulness. He is constantly thinking, and if I will only take the time to listen, I often find myself amazed.

One day I was sitting with Jacob watching a program on TV. I must admit, I was getting quite agitated with Jacob's many "Why?" "When?" "How come?" and "What will happen next?" questions. You know how it is. You can hardly concentrate on what is happening yourself because you are too busy trying to explain everything to him.

I finally received some semblance of quiet after telling Jacob to be quiet and watch the TV. This silence was soon shattered when my father stormed into the room.

"Where's my caulking gun?" he fumed. "Have you seen it?"

My father was attempting to remodel the bathroom, and at just the crucial moment he could not find his caulking gun. He was tired and frustrated, and this added hindrance was too much.

After receiving a negative reply from me, he departed from the room in much the same manner he had entered. In other words, he was mad!

A full ten minutes of glorious silence elapsed. Much to my amazement and enjoyment, Jacob had not ventured forth with even one question. I should have known better. That little mind of his was obviously working overtime. He suddenly looked up at me and broke the stillness with, "Aunt Kris, who is Papa going to kill?"

I was totally stunned. Why would Jacob think that his grandpa would want to kill anyone? Then, it hit me. To his little four-year-old mind, his question was completely logical. He had observed the facts: 1) Papa was mad. 2) Papa was looking for a gun. 3) Guns are used for killing. Therefore, the logical conclusion had to be that Papa was planning on killing someone.

I found myself laughing, but stopped when I saw the confusion enter Jacob's eyes. He had come to a very logical conclusion. How was he, a little four-year-old, supposed to know what caulking guns are used for? I had no right to laugh.

How many times have I done or said something that others have thought to be stupid or funny? Why did they call me stupid? Didn't they understand that it made sense to me? Surely they wouldn't think I would do something stupid on purpose? Believe it or not, I'm really not a stupid person. I think everything out carefully; I gather all the facts I know and then come to a conclusion. Is it my fault that some important facts are missing? How many times have I wanted to say, "Don't laugh at me. Don't call me stupid. I'm not stupid; I just did not understand. Please teach me. Explain to me where I went wrong. I know it may take a few extra minutes, but believe me, it will be well worth it. Please don't judge me too harshly. I'm learning, but many areas of my life still need a lot of growth. What I did was not stupid. It made sense to me. I just did not understand."

Little Jacob's misunderstanding presented an excellent teaching opportunity. My father soon showed Jacob a caulking gun and instructed him on its various uses. All it took was a little time. Is that too much to ask?

Sticks and Stones

When a child comes up to an adult in tears because they've been called a cruel name, what is the famous line they are usually given? I'm sure we've all heard it at one time or another: "Sticks and stones will break your bones, but words will never hurt you." This is my question: "If words cannot hurt me, then why am I in pain?"

I'd much rather have a broken arm than a broken heart. Go ahead and hit me. The cuts and bruises from sticks and stones will heal. If not, a qualified person, such as a doctor or nurse, can apply the correct medicine. This is not so with a broken heart. You cannot see a broken heart. It is impossible to see the pain which resides deep within. Many people are in pain with unseen hurts. These people (not just children) are hurting from the biting sting of careless words. Spoken words have a power that is incomprehensible.

I am not only referring to a child who has been hurt by another child. The damage caused by this is great but does not even compare to the pain which can be caused by the tongue of an adult: teacher to child, parent to child, husband to wife, wife to husband, friend to friend. The list goes on. If there were a medical plan for injuries caused by the mighty tongue, everyone would need it. Everyone has been exposed to this biting sting. Why then do we continue to use this deadly weapon in harming others?

Can you look into a child's tear-filled eyes and honestly say, "Sticks and stones will break your bones, but words will never hurt you."? If words cannot hurt, then why is the child crying? Most people would give a child more compassion if he were physically hit with sticks and stones. In fact, the child would rather have been physically hit himself. When a child is being told that words cannot hurt, not only is he being told a lie, but also he is being heaped upon with guilt that he should not be feeling this way. He is "bad" because he is crying. "Grow up, kid. Get tough! Get hard! Don't cry!" That is what he is really being told. After a while, that tender heart will get hard and stop crying – about everything. When that happens, only God can give tears to that individual. That temporary solution to tears can become permanent.

The next time we are tempted to wipe away tears with a "sticks and stones" philosophy, why don't we try a few reassuring words with a tissue? This would stop the tears, and would also soothe the pain that caused the tears.

We need to watch what we say to everyone, not just to children. James says that the tongue is an unruly evil and full of deadly poison. Poison not only hurts, it kills.

Love, Miss Hall

Little One, Little One, come now, draw near;
Open your heart and lend me your ear.
I've something to give you. My hand holds the key
That can unlock your future - your true destiny.

You yearn to be happy with a life that is rich.
You reach and you strain to find that perfect niche.
Yet, you bypass, ignore, and fail to inquire
Of the only One able to fulfill your desire.

If you only believed and understood in your heart
How deeply God loves you and yearns to impart
Unimaginable plans He has had from the start
Plans, one day revealing a great work of art.

You'd not throw them away.
Let me further explain.
What this world has to offer is empty and vain.
True satisfaction can only be found
By yielding yourself so that to Him you're bound.

He loves you! He loves you!
What more can I say?
Your tomorrow's not certain;
So seek Him today.
You *must* get to know Him by reading His Word.
That small ember inside you just needs to be stirred.

Fan the flame! Fan the flame! Then you will see
That when God controls you, you truly are free.
Free to be perfectly shaped and designed,
Free to reach out so another can find . . .

The true meaning of life.
This dark world is not all.
Will you make a difference?
Will you heed His call?
Or will you turn back?
Will you disdain His voice?
I can plead. I can cry.
But now it's your choice.

Make the right one.

Love,

Miss Hall

The Dilemma of the "Unaskable" Question

You may have heard it said that there is no such thing as a stupid question. The philosophy behind this statement is not lost on the conscientious educator. We desire to build an atmosphere in our classroom where a child will feel secure enough to ask any question he might have. In this respect, there is no such thing as a stupid question. Yet, I propose to you the dilemma of the "unaskable" question.

Imagine a child, a young boy, who, for any number of reasons, doesn't receive positive affirmation from his family. The parents may be ignorant of the boy's emotional needs; they may be preoccupied. They may even be incapable themselves of expressing encouragement, affection, praise, or even a sense of the value or worth of that boy. Therefore he may grow up with little or no positive reinforcement. Henceforth, his perspective on life will have a tendency to be one-sided. For he will receive more than enough negative feedback. You can be sure of that! This world has an abundance of that which tears down, rather than builds up. This negativity comes from children at school or in the neighborhood, inconsiderate adults, and even frustrated family members.

As this boy matures, he may be faced with the dilemma of the "unaskable" question. He may wonder if anyone truly does love him. Or he may ponder whether his life has any value at all. He may even question if he knows God or whether God could ever use him. A part of this boy does not want to believe the negative viewpoint regarding himself. Yet, how does one find out for certain? You cannot just ask such a question. For the nature of the inquiry renders any answer invalid. The mere asking of such a question places the petitioned individual in a precarious situation. Such a person is almost forced to give an affirmative answer for the sake of the one asking the question, even if it is contrary to what is true.

If this same boy, while walking down the school hallway is followed by the taunting chants of "Freak show! Freak show!" his face would burn with shame, because he is fairly certain that his tormentors are correct. How could this child ever find the courage to ask for another's perspective, knowing that his question, "Am I really a freak?" would most certainly be answered with, "Of course, not." Would anyone other than a ruthless clod ever say anything else? By asking the question, it would seem that he is asking for positive reinforcement. But what if he simply wants to know the truth? Would anyone ever answer truthfully?

Let me explain further. If the boy were to ask someone, "Do you love me?" we know that he would choose someone who was at least kind. He would not ask such a question to an enemy. Now comes the dilemma. What can a kind person say to such a question? They will invariably say, "Yes," even if "Yes," is not the truth. They are placed in a corner. Therefore, they will respond accordingly. The nature of the question actually negates the answer to the question. When a person is forced to ask any one of these "unaskable" questions, he can never be certain whether the answer he receives is valid. The fact of the matter is that the answer may well be the truth, yet the inquirer can never be certain. Some issues do not lend themselves well to inquiry. Unless someone enters this young man's life who freely expresses the positive reinforcement he craves, I fear that he may be forever searching yet never comprehending his true value.

Yes, the Bible does address these issues:

God tells us of the depths of His love for us in John 3:16:

"For God so loved the world, that he gave his only begotten Son, that whosoever believeth in him should not perish, but have everlasting life."

He tells us that He is on our side in Psalm 56:9b:

". . . this I know; for God is for me."

He reveals to us our value as His creation in Psalm 139:14

"I will praise thee; for I am fearfully and wonderfully made: marvellous are thy works; and that my soul knoweth right well."

Nevertheless, a person who has not received this affirmation from people has a difficult time accepting it from God.

What can I, as a Christian educator, do to alleviate this dilemma? I can determine that every child under my instruction will hear the answer to life's "unaskable" questions before those questions can even darken the mind. I can make sure that my students know the answers, whether or not they need them. I can constantly affirm to my students how valuable they are because they *are* of great value. I can tell them how much God desires to use them because He *does* desire to use them. I can show them that they are loved because they *are* loved.

The Annoying Noise

It happened during Bible class. Teaching as I normally would, I stood behind my podium with my books for other subjects sitting on the table beside the podium. I was totally lost in my Bible story when I hear it ... a continual squeaking noise. At first, I attempted to ignore it. Surely, it was accidentally made and would stop on its own. I went on with my lesson only to find myself distracted again. I looked around trying to make eye contact with the offending student in order to give them that "teacher look" that says, "Please don't do that." I did not want to have to interrupt my lesson to care for this minute problem. Try as I might, I could not find the fidgeter. The noise seemed to grow in intensity. No longer able to ignore it, I stopped teaching and said, "Whoever is squeaking their desk, please stop. I am sure that you are not even aware that you were making noises, but please sit still as it is very distracting." Surely, now the problem was cared for. I again continued with my lesson, and the squeaking resumed as well. Now I was getting angry. The noise had to be annoying others as well as me. This had to stop! I again addressed the issue. Speaking very sharply, I said, "This noise will stop! *Now* you're just being disobedient. You know who you are. If you continue to disturb the class in this manner, you will be in major trouble!" Most of my students by this time looked truly concerned. I, myself, could not believe that I had in my class such an impudent student.

Although I had threatened and cajoled, nothing I did seemed to have any effect on the perpetrator. Finally, I resorted to desperate measures. I was going to ferret out this troublemaker once and for all! This time I told my students that someone had to know who was making this noise. I needed them to tell me who it was right now!

As I looked around at my room full of wide-eyed faces, I saw one little hand very tentatively rise. What a relief! Finally, I would be able to resolve this situation and continue my lesson. When I acknowledged this brave ten-year-old, she very reluctantly pointed to my podium. Consumed with my lesson, I had inadvertently been jiggling my foot. This motion caused the podium to rub against the adjoining table, thereby resulting in a screeching noise.

Now, what was I to do? Not only had I almost succeeded in driving myself crazy and wasted many precious minutes, but I had blamed it all on my innocent students.

After a few minutes of intense silence, I could tell that the class was beginning to burst at the seams with contained laughter. How could I escape from this mess with what little dignity which remained? I had two choices. I could try to put a lid on the situation and pretend nothing ever happened, or I could laugh at myself with them, admitting to having been a fool. Have you ever been there?

It may appear to be an insignificant matter; yet, in reality, my response to this situation was very important. How often have I admonished my students that how they respond to a situation is often what really matters? I teach them how they ought to react when corrected, how they ought to respond when bothered by others, when frustrated, when angry, etc. I tell them that I don't expect them to be perfect, but I do expect them to own up when they mess up. How often my tendency is to do just the opposite. I'm the teacher. I have dignity. I have a reputation to keep. I have to be perfect.

The fact is, my students don't want a teacher who is perfect. What they want (and need) is a teacher who is real, a teacher who practices what she preaches, a teacher who, when she messes up, and it affects the students 'fesses up. Students need a teacher who is not above apologizing to a student when that student was wrongly accused or wrongly punished.

We all mess up sometimes. And, in reality, we don't lose something when we admit that we messed up. We actually gain something. We gain our students' respect, and we show them that we respect them. Very few adults ever tell a child that they are sorry for wronging them. Maybe we are just too proud. We also gain a connection with that child – a relationship that is just a bit stronger than before. A child has seen our frailty, our humanness; has heard our admission; and has seen us dust ourselves off and go on.

Isn't that what all of life involves? Are we not constantly having to do the same with God? He doesn't expect us to be perfect. He knows who we are. He knows that we are nothing but dust. He expects us to 'fess up when we mess up, and then pick ourselves up and go on.

Are you wondering how I handled the situation of the annoying noise? Actually, I think I handled it properly ... that time. Although, I must admit, that has not always been the case. I laughed, and I let them laugh until the giggles were all gone. It was funny, even though the joke was on me. And it was okay. For they didn't need a teacher who was perfect. They just needed one who was real.

Please, Feed the Birds

A little over a year ago, I moved here from the cold north. It is cold in temperature, yes; but the coldness which affected me the most was the coldness of hospitality. I had lived there for fifteen years and had been able to give my heart to influence many children and families. I truly loved my church and my job, but I was hungry. I was not even certain of the object of my hunger until one of the first Sundays here in Arkansas. I was invited to a friend's house for dinner. As I sat around the table and we bowed our heads to pray, I began to cry. I realized exactly then what I had been needing. Although I am quite content being single and quite satisfied with the love of friends and distant family, my soul was starving due to lack of fellowship and camaraderie that comes with being part of a family. For many years, I knew that I had dreaded Sundays; yet I didn't know why. I knew every Sunday as I sat quietly in my home eating dinner alone that I was missing something. Yet I wasn't sure what it was. I realized it that day at the house of my friend. Up north, people I knew, even good friends of mine, tended to guard their family time. How I yearned for a little morsel of that sense of belonging, that sense of companionship. That day at dinner, I was fed. In fact, I was completely satisfied before the meal had even begun.

Hunger is a God-given response to a need in our life. People are hungry for many things other than food. Some may need encouragement. Others may need acceptance, love, or even attention - that reassurance that their life matters. Often people are not even aware of the thing for which they hunger. They just feel that emptiness and look for ways to fill it. Children are no exception. Many of the children in our classrooms are hungry, yet they have no idea what will satisfy their hunger. Although I am sure that it is God's plan that most of these childhood needs be filled through a loving, nurturing, family environment; sadly, often this is not the case. For whatever reason, even good Christian parents fail to satisfy some basic needs of their children. Often parents are only beginning to learn how to be good Christians, much less good parents. Is it any wonder that some children come to us starving?

What are we as Christian school teachers to do? The need seems so great. It is almost overwhelming at times. One thing we can do is to be very liberal, not in our politics but with our encouragement and affection. The children who get all they need at home won't be hungry, but that starving child will soak it all up. Also, we must realize that we really don't know who it is that is hungry. Some children let us know, but others may not give any sign at all. Don't assume that children from **good church families** don't need our attention. Freely distribute your food to all, or you may miss that one who desperately needs you.

My mother got saved when I was four years old. From that time until I was eleven, we went to church sporadically. My mother yearned to have a good Christian home, but my father, though saved, wasn't really interested in church. One Saturday, while I was in the fifth grade, my father said that we were going to a new church the next day. My mother, who had just broken her foot, didn't attend with us. Within three months we had joined the church and our family has attended regularly ever since. My father quickly became a deacon and a bus driver in this growing church. My mother became a Sunday school teacher and director of a girls' singing group. We became a church family. We were considered a pillar in the church. And yet, my parents were still learning. The fact is most parents tend to rear their children in the manner in which they themselves were reared unless godly training intervenes. Henceforth, many mothers and fathers are destined to repeat the mistakes of their own parents.

I know that all little children are cuddly and huggable. So, I am sure, as a baby, I probably had my share of hugs. Yet, as a child, I was hungry. In fact, from the earliest of my memories until I was perhaps fifteen or sixteen, I remember receiving only one hug. It was given to me by my third-grade public school teacher. I really didn't know how to respond to it. I am sure I was stiff as a board and definitely didn't hug her back. I didn't even know I needed a hug. All I knew was that my teacher satisfied an emptiness deep within me. I didn't quite understand it then, but I never forgot it.

We have such an opportunity as teachers in a Christian school. We are allowed to influence so many lives, yet sometimes we think we know who needs that little bit of extra attention and who doesn't. In fact, often we haven't a clue. I picture my distribution of affection in my classroom as a person sitting on a park bench tossing out seed to hungry birds. I can't know with any certainty which bird is truly hungry and which one is just there for a little snack. Only by liberally distributing the seed to all the birds can I be sure that the starving one gets what it needs. As with birdseed, my love, encouragement, praise, and attention must be distributed freely. To the child who is full, my words will be like dessert. It tastes good, yet it is not altogether necessary. But the starving child will grasp my words, hold them close to his heart, and savor them for weeks, maybe even years to come. I want to do all that I can to feed the birds. I don't want one soul to wander away empty.

Possessing the Tools

Early every morning the man boarded the commuter train. This specific train was his means of transportation to work. His job involved maintenance work for a large corporation. Although any cumbersome equipment needed for his employment remained at his main plant, he always kept his personal toolbox, a special gift from his parents, by his side (much as a doctor carries a medical bag). These tools were his own property. He preferred using them whenever necessary.

One morning, as this man entered the train, his eyes were inadvertently drawn to a screw which had worked its way loose from some operational apparatus on the train. He hesitated and then continued back to his regular seat. He knew that it would be a simple and painless procedure to withdraw one of his tools (in this instance, a screwdriver) from his ever-present bag and tighten the screw. It would only take a minute. But this was not his responsibility. Sure, he was qualified and even had the proper tools, yet he was certain that someone else would care for this minor problem. Besides, he had planned on catching a quick nap on his ride into work this morning. He had been up awfully late the previous evening.

Day after day, the same scene was repeated. The part of the scene which differed was that the screw grew continuously looser, and the man had an endless succession of endeavors to occupy his time during his commute to work. Some days he read the paper; other days, he visited with friends. He always attempted to stay busy. He never failed to notice the screw, but he was pacified in the knowledge that whoever was responsible would notice the problem and take care of the situation. He possessed the ability and the tools; he even saw the need. Nevertheless, he figured that someone else would right the situation. Would he have acted immediately if he had realized the dangling screw was a vital part of the braking mechanism to this particular commuter train?

A child is enrolled in a Christian school by loving parents who desire the best for their offspring. Day after day, year after year, the child is trained to live a life pleasing to God. He is taught much more than general academics. He is given various Bible truths and life lessons. He is warned of the pitfalls of sin. He is saturated with the Word of God. Through daily recitation, he has committed hundreds of Bible verses to memory. He is shown how to know God.

By the age of twelve, this child is equipped with more knowledge of God than most adults in this world. This child has been given an invaluable gift to carry with him always. He is the recipient of tools with which he will be able to make a difference in this weary world. His parents and teachers have equipped him well. He cannot fail to see the need. He passes by the need each day as multitudes of unwary commuters race on a terrifying ride straight toward eternity. Will he step out of himself and be willing to use his tools to help save another's life?

Or will he be content to sit idly by, possessing the means of salvation? Will he wait for another to see the need?

Is it nothing to you, all ye that pass by? …

A Glimpse of a Teacher's Heart

This selection is an excerpt of a letter written to introduce herself to the administrator of the Christian school at which she would eventually teach for her last ten years. We include it here because as she introduces herself to this school, we can catch a glimpse of her heart and motivation for her life's purpose. Anything personal or not relevant to learning of the heart of the teacher has been omitted. The letter is dated July 20, 2003.

"Dear Bro. Eric,

" . . . it occurred to me that most of what you know about me comes second-hand.

" . . . I thought it might help if I introduced you to the real Kristen Hall.

1. I am a teacher. God made me to be a teacher. He gave me the "heart" and the necessary abilities to be able to teach. I think I do a good job. I've not had many complaints. You would have to ask my pastor or principal to know for sure. I have taught upper elementary classes for fourteen years. I believe that being a teacher allows me the opportunity to influence children in many areas of life. My goals are to encourage and inspire children:

A. To realize that God created each person uniquely, and He wants to do something special with each life

B. To prepare themselves with a willing heart and a clean life so that God will be able to use them abundantly

C. To love reading

D. To appreciate and enjoy God's awesome creation

E. To awaken a thirst to learn and to enjoy learning

F. To realize that history is not a boring subject; it is rather quite fascinating

G. To learn how to respond properly in many situations

H. To know that God really, truly loves them

2. I have worked for eleven years with junior camp ~ three years as a counselor and eight years as assistant cook.
3. I enjoy designing bookmarks, cards, programs, etc. on the computer.
4. I enjoy singing in choir and in groups.

. . .

(5.) I wish that I knew God better.

(6.) I get great satisfaction out of expressing my thoughts and emotions in writing.

(7.) I am very close to my family.

" . . . I am content with my job right now and the thought of packing up and starting all over again to earn the trust of new parents seems a little daunting at best . . .

"If you find that a person with my abilities can fill a need in your ministry, please give me a call.

Sincerely,

Kristen M. Hall"

Sixth Grade Contemplation

My heart was filled with trepidation
As I began my preparation
For this new phase of education.
Was a 6th Grade class for me?

I would need to know much information:
Diagrams for identification,
Rules to teach of punctuation.
Was a 6th Grade class for me?

My students were a combination,
A variation of civilization.
Could I give each one a good foundation?
Was a 6th Grade class for me?

Then I gazed with earnest captivation
At Jacob's colorful imagination,
Nick T.'s and Steve's determination,
David's unbroken concentration,
Stephanie's thoughtful consideration,
Kelsey Horton's cooperation,
Nathan, with his procrastination
(Which did improve with much motivation),
Ashley's melodic instrumentation,
Christopher's knack for observation,
Tara's ready participation,
Kayla and Kate with their jubilation
(Especially regarding communication),
Corey's and Nick K.'s imitation
Of each other for some recreation
(Much to my constant exasperation),

Kelsey Peckham's dedication
Without a moment's hesitation,
Tiffany's wonderful qualification
Of behaving herself in any location,
Michael's many an illustration,
And Emily's vibrant appreciation.

After much investigation,
These all have earned my high commendation.
And, in this, my current estimation,
Deserve a sincere congratulation
With celebration and orchestration.
Also, with hearty recommendation,
for all of their great implementation,
I wish them each one a stupendous vacation.
This 6th Grade class WAS for me!

Miss Hall

The Teacher / Student Connection

(A Meeting of the Heart)

"My son, give me thine heart, and let thine eyes observe my ways." Prov. 23:26

As a child, do you remember how you felt on the first day of school each year? Do you remember the excitement of getting your school supplies in order? Everything was fresh and new. Do you recall wondering about your new teacher? Your new class? Your new classmates? I know, for me, my biggest question was always, "Will I like my teacher?," and, more importantly, "Will she like me?" Invariably, the ones who I thought liked me were always the ones I liked the best.

When I look back over my many years of school, the good years were good because I believed my teacher cared about me. The bad years were bad because I believed my teacher did not like me at all. Notice, those good and bad years were not dependent on friends, subject matter, or field trips but on teachers. What an incredible responsibility!

Was my childish mind always right regarding my teacher's heart? Maybe not. But does it really matter whether I was right or wrong? Isn't it more important that a child know for certain that his or her teacher thinks that child is something special? Therefore, in order to make that heart connection, you must love each child deeply and be able to express that love in acceptable ways.

If you have been around people very long, you have certainly noticed that not all people are naturally easy to love. It is the same with children. While some children knit with us easily, we may find others difficult to even like. How then can we love each student individually? This is an impossible task unless we allow God to love them through us. For God does love each child with a perfect, unselfish love. He created each one, has a plan for each one, and died for each one.

We must pray that God would love each student through us. For He truly does love them! We, as teachers, can be instruments of that love. When we try to see that difficult child as God sees him, when we "look through God's eyes," we can't help but love him. Also remember, the difficult child that **knows** his teacher loves him tends to at least **try** to be more cooperative. A child who tries to obey yet fails is much easier to deal with than the one who never tries at all.

Upon entering Christian education in the ninth grade, the first Scripture passage I was required to memorize was I Corinthians 13. Once I learned it, I never forgot it. I never realized then that that passage would give me the confidence to pursue a teaching career. I had just completed student teaching yet felt totally inadequate to teach. I had never done well in speech class. To this day, whenever I get nervous, my brain freezes up making communication extremely difficult. While driving alone one day, I decided to quote Scripture that I had at one time committed to memory. As I quoted I Corinthians 13, the words pierced my heart. This passage is vital for anyone striving to influence people, especially teachers.

"Though I speak with the tongues of men and of angels, and have not charity, I am become as sounding brass or a tinkling cymbal."

Wow! I don't have to be the most eloquent speaker to be effective. I just have to love my students. It is good to speak properly, but if I do not communicate through love, my words are empty. They may touch the head but not the heart.

"And though I have the gift of prophecy, and understand all mysteries, and all knowledge, and though I have all faith so that I could remove mountains, and have not charity, I am nothing."

As important as studying is, all those hard-sought-after facts are all in vain if I don't truly care about the person to whom I am giving them.

"And though I bestow all my goods to feed the poor, and though I give my body to be burned, and have not charity, it profiteth me nothing."

So much sacrifice yet all done for naught if I am not motivated by love.

"Charity suffereth long, and is kind:"

If I truly love my students, even when pushed to the limits, I will remain kind. How convicting!

"Charity envieth not; charity vaunteth not itself, is not puffed up, doth not behave itself unseemly, seeketh not her own,"

It is so sad when we find ourselves in competition with other teachers. We want to be the most popular. We want to be the most beloved. We want to keep our good ideas to ourselves so that we look good. Is this the purpose of teaching?

"is not easily provoked, thinketh no evil; Rejoiceth not in iniquity, but rejoiceth in the truth; Beareth all things, believeth all things ..."

Quite convicting, isn't it? Am I allowing that troubled child to "get on my last nerve"? Am I annoyed because he is making me to have a bad day? I'm there for him. I am to be what he needs. He is not in my class for my benefit. I am commanded to love him no matter what he does.

"... hopeth all things, endureth all things."

If I love my students, I will **never** give up on them. I will continue to hope even when it seems impractical to do so.

"Charity never faileth: but whether there be prophecies, they shall fail; whether there be tongues, they shall cease; whether there be knowledge, it shall vanish away."

Truly caring about my students is a sure thing. God's love **will not** fail. It will not fail to touch a heart, a life, a future.

"For we know in part, and we prophesy in part. But when that which is perfect is come, then that which is in part shall be done away. When I was a child, I spake as a child, I understood as a child, I thought as a child: but when I became a man, I put away childish things. For now we see through a glass, darkly; but then face to face: now I know in part; but then shall I know even as also I am known. And now abideth faith, hope, charity, these three; but the greatest of these is charity."

I may not be the greatest speaker. I may not be the most intelligent educator. I may not have attained the highest level of learning. But I can love my students. Can you?

The Teacher / Student Connection

Part II

Teacher, Do You Love Me?

(and other questions from a child's heart)

"My son, give me thine heart, and let thine eyes observe my ways." Prov. 23:26

Do you remember the excitement of the first day of school? You are eager to be back with your friends after a long summer. You have all your new school supplies, your new lunch box, your new clothes, and your new book bag. You also have a new year, a fresh start. The only uncertainty is that all-important tool of education: your teacher. What will he or she be like? A teacher is that one ingredient that can make or break a school year. The purpose of this writing is to encourage you, the teacher, to take the effort required in order to make a heart connection with each child in your classroom.

I. Will my teacher like me?
   (love)
II. Will my teacher be boring?
   (passion for teaching)
III. Will my teacher make me obey?
   (discipline)
IV. Will my teacher think I'm important?
   (encouragement)
V. Will my teacher be fair?
   (consistency)

VI.   Will my teacher be real?
       (transparency)
VII.   Will my teacher protect me?
       (compassion)
VIII. Will my teacher make school fun?
       (enjoyment of life)

Connect through **love** with prayer for each child. Ask God to love your students through you. Be a conduit of His love. Learn I Corinthians 13. Even the most difficult child will be more cooperative if he feels cared about. Children can be forgiving of your mistakes if they believe you truly care.

Connect through **encouragement** with praise for each child. Most children truly want to please. They need to know when they have succeeded. Pointing out the good often makes the good continue. Every individual needs praise. Praise their good work and their good character. This world is a very negative place. Some children come to us very beaten down. A child needs to understand how valuable he is to God. We need to see the child the way God sees him and then communicate that to the child.

Connect through your **enjoyment of life** with personal illustrations. Children love to hear that you were once a kid and that you remember how it feels to be young. Use your own childhood incidents as examples: fear, disobedience, embarrassment, friends. You can also use present-day examples. Use simple incidents that you have learned from but retain professionalism.

Examples:

> I watched the sunset.
> I saw a rainbow yesterday.
> Share answered prayers.
> Share prayer requests that are not too personal (sick family member).

Share your **passion for teaching** through reading. If you do not already have a love for reading, get one! If you love it, they will, too! Choose books you love. Choose books that teach good character lessons. Choose books that touch the heart. Such a great connection can be gained by sharing a good book with another person. Choose books at an appropriate grade level / interest level. Some books may be above their reading level but not above their interest level. Choose books that reinforce your history lessons.

Set a time to read. It should last approximately fifteen minutes. I have found the best times are during a scheduled fruit break or right after recess when the children are a little tired. I allow the students to rest their heads. I have always told them that they do not have to listen, but they may not keep someone else from listening. They may sleep, if they choose, but they may not snore. Most will listen intently if you have chosen an appropriate book.

Use your voice to hold the students' attention. This may be difficult when you read a book aloud for the first time, but use different voices for different characters. Stop at the exciting points to build anticipation. Make comments periodically and ask questions.

> "I can't believe he is going to do that!"
> "What do you think is going to happen?"

So many concepts can be taught simply by experiencing situations in a book. More importantly, hearts can be connected by sharing a story.

Connect through **transparency** by being real. When you blow it, 'fess up. Children are very forgiving. If you offend a child, ask for forgiveness. Tell them your vision for them. These should be natural statements from you:

"I want so much for you to know how much God loves you."
"I want so much for you to know how much God wants to use you."
"I want you to know how important you are to God."
"I desire for you to know God."

Remind your students that you are always learning. Tell them things which you have learned.
Children want to know 1) that you love them, 2) that you are real, and 3) that you think they are a person of value. The academics, as important as they are, are tools in teaching how to live. A child that receives straight A's yet has no perceived value in his life is a failure. We must influence all children through connecting with their heart. We want to give them tools that go beyond the mind; tools that reach the heart.

What Are You Teaching?

This is an outline to a devotional that I have heard Kristen give a few times when we were teaching together. I did not wish to "ad-lib" or say something that Kristen did not say. I also did not wish to leave it out just because it isn't polished. It is a valuable lesson that I am afraid we as teachers sometimes do not realize we are teaching. So here it is, bare bones. Let us be willing to take it to heart and learn a lesson about ourselves.

- As a college student, I knew that I liked biology. Most children we teach have not yet been exposed to a subject enough to know if they have an inclination toward that subject.

- It is wrong for us, as teachers, to ruin the fascination of learning for our students because some sad teacher in our past ruined it for us. (history)

- Our approach to a subject will often determine a student's attitude toward that subject for the remainder of his life.

- Are we using our influence wisely?
- Sunrises / Sunsets
- Andrew
- What else have I taught without realizing it?
- What are we really teaching in our classrooms? Whatever it is, I can guarantee they are getting it.

Let Your Circle Be Enlarged

The life of Joseph amazes me. He had many devastating events happen to him that could have easily destroyed him, yet he succeeded in focusing on the big picture. How did he do it? He did not have any of the devices that I cling to when I face my petty problems. He did not have a godly friend to give him a pep talk when he got discouraged. He did not have a loving family whom he knew would be disappointed if he fell by the wayside. He did not even have a Bible where he could find comfort.

"And we know that all things work together for good to them that love God, to them who are the called according to his purpose." Romans 8:28

How did Joseph keep from "throwing in the towel"?

I can only find three things that Joseph had that might have kept him encouraged. First of all, the Bible says:

"... the Lord was with him and ... made all that he did to prosper." Genesis 39:3

Joseph realized that in the pit, in those slave quarters, even in that cold, dark prison, he was not alone. God was with him. Even though it appeared as though all others had forsaken him, somehow he could sense the presence of God.

Secondly, Joseph had his father's faith. That same God who wrestled all night with his father, that same God who visited with his father at Bethel, that same God who guided and protected his father, was at his disposal, too. If Jacob could trust God, then so could Joseph. He held on to his father's faith.

Finally, Joseph had his dreams. He knew that those dreams meant something. Although his brothers mocked them and even his father questioned the validity of them, still Joseph held those dreams to his heart. He clung to the fact that God was in control and had a greater purpose for Joseph's life.

In spite of all his difficulties, Joseph refused to get bitter, refused to throw his life away to immorality, and refused to give in to the paralysis of self-pity.

While I am amazed at Joseph, I am often disgusted with my response to the small difficulties in my own life. Actually, I probably respond better with the major problems in my life. It seems to be the small matters that cause me to stumble the most.

I have here a small illustration that I use in my class every year. This strip of paper represents God's purpose for my life, my sphere of influence for Him, and the love and care He has for me. As you notice, when I connect the ends of my paper, I now have a circle of paper containing GOD and ME.

Now enters a little kink in my life: a trouble, a difficulty, a concern. (Begin cutting paper.) It might be that the problem is financial. I am fine with the situation until a little voice in my ear says, "Does God really see what is going on here? Does He realize how hard I am working? Does He really care that I am going through this?" It isn't the problem that can destroy me; it is my response to the situation that does the damage.

Or the problem might be as simple as having to wear nylons that I cannot afford to buy. Or it may be purchasing a new pair of nylons only to put my finger through them the first time I try to wear them. That little voice begins talking again.

There may be times when I've worked arduously on a project only to have someone else get the credit. I might feel unappreciated. Again, that little voice whispers to me: "God is not really interested in what you do. Your life is not that important to Him. Anyone can do what you do."

As long as I focus on God and the big picture, I am fine; but as soon as I begin listening to that silky voice, I begin to sink. I then no longer want to look at the big picture. I no longer want to spend time with God.

Any difficulty I have, small or large, cannot destroy the purpose for my life, my sphere of influence, or the love and care God has for me. Remember, God is in control of every circumstance of my life. If something happens to me God has allowed it to happen for some reason. I don't have to understand it; I just have to trust Him and obey Him.

As difficulties and problems continue my way, Satan will constantly try to use them to destroy God's purpose for my life. Sometimes it would almost seem as if he might win. One more cut is all it will take. When I make this final cut, what will I then have? (Finish cutting the strip.) Satan has won, right? Or has he?

Wow! What do I have? Instead of two individual circles, I now have one larger one. The circle is still intact. God doesn't allow things into our lives to harm us. He desires to broaden our influence, to use us in a bigger way, to deepen our dependence on Him.

You may wonder how I accomplished this "trick." That is the beauty of this illustration. I know how to make it turn out the right way, yet I don't understand why it works. You see, before I attached the ends of my strip of paper, I placed a twist in the paper. That little kink makes me change planes (that's a geometric term) as I am cutting. Therefore, I end up with a larger circle instead of two small ones every time. I don't understand why. If I end where I began, my brain says that I should have two circles. I don't understand why it works, but I do understand how to make it work. Isn't that how Romans 8:28 is? We may not understand it, but if we focus on loving God and doing what we know He wants us to do, He can use the difficulties in our life to develop the big picture.

Five Smooth Stones

Here is another thought-provoking outline. These are some really good points to use in developing either a lesson or a teachers' devotional.

Why smooth stones?

1. Sure aim
2. Less resistance
3. More usable

How is a rock smoothed?

1. Tumbling
2. Water and sand
3. Constant pressure / friction
4. Edges worn off

You, Too, Can Teach

This is the outline Kristen used when addressing the student teachers who learned in our classrooms before graduating from Christian college.

- Why I love teaching
- How long before I realized I had a gift
- As a college student, how can I begin to understand the bigness of teaching?
- What God has placed in your heart as a teacher
- Working with disabled children, especially those with dysfunctional behavior
    - lazy
    - manipulative
    - bully
    - needy
- Pray, pray, pray!
    - wisdom - Proverbs
    - love – I Corinthians 13, dysfunctional student
- Incorporate two or three elementary teaching methods in teaching this college level class.
- The awesomeness of teaching
- Me, a teacher? You, a teacher? (You will teach in some capacity.)

- I build children.
  - Character
  - Encouragement
    - You can!
    - Don't waste your life!
    - God wants to use you!
  - Skills
    - Math
    - Language
    - Reading
  - Fascination with learning / children have a natural curiosity
  - Information
- I teach with my life.

Ten Commandments for Teachers

Thou shalt be content.
Let your conversation be without covetousness; and be content with such things as ye have: for He hath said, I will never leave thee, nor forsake thee.
Hebrews 13:5

But godliness with contentment is great gain.
I Timothy 6:6

Thou shalt be faithful.
He that is faithful in that which is least is faithful also in much:
and he that is unjust in the least is unjust also in much.
Luke 16:10

Moreover it is required in stewards, that a man be found faithful.
I Corinthians 4:2

Thou shalt be patient.
Be patient therefore, brethren, unto the coming of the Lord. Behold, the husbandman waiteth for the precious fruit of the earth, and hath long patience for it, until he receive the early and latter rain. Be ye also patient; stablish your hearts: for the coming of the Lord draweth nigh.
James 5:7-8

Thou shalt have a sense of humor.

A merry heart doeth good like a medicine: but a broken spirit drieth the bones.

Proverbs 17:22

Thou shalt be flexible.

And let the peace of God rule in your hearts, to the which also ye are called in one body; and be ye thankful.

Colossians 3:15

Thou shalt be teachable.

He that refuseth instruction despiseth his own soul: but he that heareth reproof getteth understanding.

Proverbs 15:32

Thou shalt be a servant.

Let as many servants as are under the yoke count their own masters worthy of all honor, that the name of God and his doctrine be not blasphemed.

I Timothy 6:1

Thou shalt be dependable.

In all things shewing thyself a pattern of good works: in doctrine shewing uncorruptness, gravity, sincerity,

Titus 2:7

Thou shalt be loyal.
Then said Jesus unto his disciples,
If any man will come after me, let him deny himself, and
take up his cross, and follow me.
Matthew 16:24-25

Thou shalt not gossip.
And withal they learn to be idle, wandering about from
house to house; and not only idle,
but tattlers also and busybodies, speaking things which
they ought not.
I Timothy 5:13

The

Shadow

of a Legacy

Kristen Hall taught students at two schools during her lifetime. The first, where she began her career straight out of college, was State Line Christian School (**SLCS**), in Temperance, Michigan, on the state line bordering Toledo, Ohio. Here she developed her calling and talents; here she forged lifetime friendships; here her incredible influence began.

The second, and last, was Gospel Light Christian School (**GLCS**), in Hot Springs, Arkansas. Here she perfected her calling and talents; here she rekindled college friendships while also making new ones; here her incredible influence continues; and here, her legacy lives on.

A few of her former students would like to share their thoughts about this tremendous teacher.

Abby (Worley) Bennett, Nurse, former student, SLCS:

Miss Hall gave me a love for reading! She poured her whole heart into her students. Miss Hall was a wonderful, godly example to her students. I will never forget the books she would read to us about missionaries and people who influenced America's history. She is exactly the teacher I aspire to be. Thank you, Miss Hall for LOVING your students!

Mike Meade, former student, SLCS:

Miss Hall, you just had something different than all my other teachers. Other teachers just seemed to have a routine with every day. You made each day fun! You seemed to enjoy teaching and showed it amazingly. Thanks for being an awesome teacher.

Corey Horn, former student, SLCS:

My heart is heavy since my favorite grade-school teacher has gone to Heaven. She told me I could be anything I wanted to be. She taught a lot about life.

Megan Dukeshire, former student, GLCS:

The best thing in fourth grade was all the books she read. I loved my teacher, Miss Hall.

Kelsey Johnson, Aspiring Teacher, former student, GLCS: "Memories of A Remarkable Teacher"

Miss Hall was, without a doubt, the best teacher I ever had. I remember growing up, two of my three older siblings had her as a teacher, and they would talk about what an awesome teacher she was along with the great books she would read to the class. When I finally reached the fifth grade, I was ecstatic; and that truly was my best year of elementary. She is the reason I now love history, and I have continued to love books. For basically the whole duration of being in her class, I was absorbed in books of WWII and the Holocaust. My mom once told me that she had asked Miss Hall if she should be worried of my interest in such a morbid part of history, and she just said something to the effect of, "No, she is just like me." After my Mom told me about this conversation, I remember feeling a sense of pride being compared to such a remarkable woman by Miss Hall herself. I was lucky to have her for both my fifth and sixth grade years. She was diagnosed with cancer my sixth-grade year, which was pretty tough on all of us; but she was a fighter and she continued coming to class as often as she could.

My sixth-grade year is when I first took an interest in photography. I look back and laugh at the poor quality of the photos, but I also smile tearfully at the memories captured on that thirty-dollar camera. My experiences in those two short years are one of the main reasons I will be majoring in elementary education after I graduate this year. Miss Hall is proof of how much one person can impact so many. Her godly and positive influence will always be a major part of my childhood.

Abby (McGowan) McCreight, EMT, former student, GLCS:

I remember when Miss Hall came to our school. My sisters had her as a teacher first, and I remember hearing about all the fun stuff she would do in class. I couldn't wait to have her as a teacher! The day finally came for her to be my sixth-grade teacher. I was so excited!

She would always start the day off with prayer, a devotional, and singing. She had the best song selection, and everyone had their turn to pick out what songs we would sing that day. My favorite was "How Can I Fear?" by Ron Hamilton.

She had her own library where we could check out books. I never enjoyed reading before, but there was something about checking out one of Miss Hall's books that made reading fun. I would always ask about the people that checked out the book before me, and she would always tell me about them. She remembered all of her students.

She always read to us after lunch. I loved to hear her read. She made all the stories come to life. It was the highlight of my day.

There's so much more I could say about Miss Hall, but the most important thing about her is the impact she had on my life. I think about her often and hum the songs we used to sing in her class. I think about the competitive games we would play, the butterflies each of us had, and so much more. You knew she loved Jesus, her family, her students, and Eeyore. I miss her. I am so blessed to have had her as a teacher.

The Most Important Legacy

Thank you for honoring my friend by reading her thoughts. If you have made any decisions as a result of this manuscript, I would sincerely like to know about them.

If you have any specific questions or concerns with which I could help you or any prayer requests to share, I would certainly appreciate the opportunity to be a blessing.

I can best be contacted by e-mail through my company:

superiorscholasticskills@gmail.com

Kristen Hall dedicated her life to teaching children in the Christian school. Most of these writings are designed to help students and teachers alike become better Christians and to develop our influence to help others become better Christians. Perhaps you may be reading these selections and have never become a Christian. If that is the case, and you are not sure of a home in Heaven someday, please continue reading the Scripture selections on the following page:

1. We do not deserve Heaven: *"For all have sinned, and come short of the glory of God." – Romans 3:23.* At one time or another, we have all chosen to disobey God.

2. Our sin has a penalty: *"For the wages {payment} of sin is death; but the gift of God is eternal life through Jesus Christ our Lord." – Romans 6:23.* The payment for our disobedience is spiritual death and Hell. (Matthew 25:46, Revelation 21:8)

3. Jesus paid our penalty. *"But God commendeth {proved} His love toward us, in that, while we were yet sinners, Christ died for us." – Romans 5:8.* God proved His love for us by giving His only Son to die on the cross for our sin. Jesus rose again the third day *{Easter}*, conquered death and Hell and paid our penalty for sin.

4. We must believe on Jesus and accept His payment for our sin: *"That if thou shalt confess with thy mouth the Lord Jesus, and shalt believe in thine heart that God hath raised Him from the dead, thou shalt be saved." – Romans 10:9.* To believe on Jesus Christ as your Saviour means to have faith that He died for you, paid the price for your sin, and is **the only** way to Heaven. You can express your belief in Jesus through prayer, but it is the faith and belief that assures you of His acceptance. There are no "magic words."

5. Pray sincerely after this example: "Dear Jesus, I know that I am a sinner and do not deserve Heaven. I believe that You died on the cross, paid the penalty for my sin, and rose again after three days. I am placing my faith and trust in You alone to forgive my sin and take me to Heaven when I die. Thank You for Your gift of eternal life! In Jesus' name, Amen."